ZAXON MOONRAKER

A Police Dog's Tale

By

Mal Nutbrown

Copyright © Mal Nutbrown 2023
This book is sold subject to the condition that it shall not, by way of trade or otherwise, be lent, resold, hired out, or otherwise circulated without the publisher's prior consent in any form of binding or cover other than that in which it is published and without a similar condition including this condition being imposed on the subsequent publisher.
The moral right of Mal Nutbrown has been asserted.

While all the stories in this book are true, some names and identifying details have been changed to protect the privacy of the people involved.

DEDICATION

This tale is a tribute to my beloved family: Elizabeth, Claire and Tom. Each of you have been such a brilliant light in my life and I owe so much to your unquestioning love and support. I hope that through this story, you may come to see how hard it was for me at times and understand why my moods could take such sudden shifts, or why I had moments of complete disregard for the issues in your lives. It is also dedicated to my four wonderful grandchildren who will hopefully learn a little more about their grumpy grandad.

I am eternally grateful to my parents, my mum Betty and my late dad Ian, for all their unwavering love and sound guidance as I was growing up. They gave me the tools to think independently and make confident decisions in adulthood. Oh, and Dad – thank you for gifting me your crackpot sense of humour; it's helped me through many difficult moments.

I am particularly indebted to Zac, not only for his unwavering loyalty and courage but also for being a loyal companion and a delight to work with over such a long period of time. He was with me through good times and bad, never failing to offer comfort and protection when needed. No matter what I do or say, I will never be able to truly thank him adequately for his incomparable friendship.

Thank you from the bottom of my heart, Zac. You will live on in my soul forever!

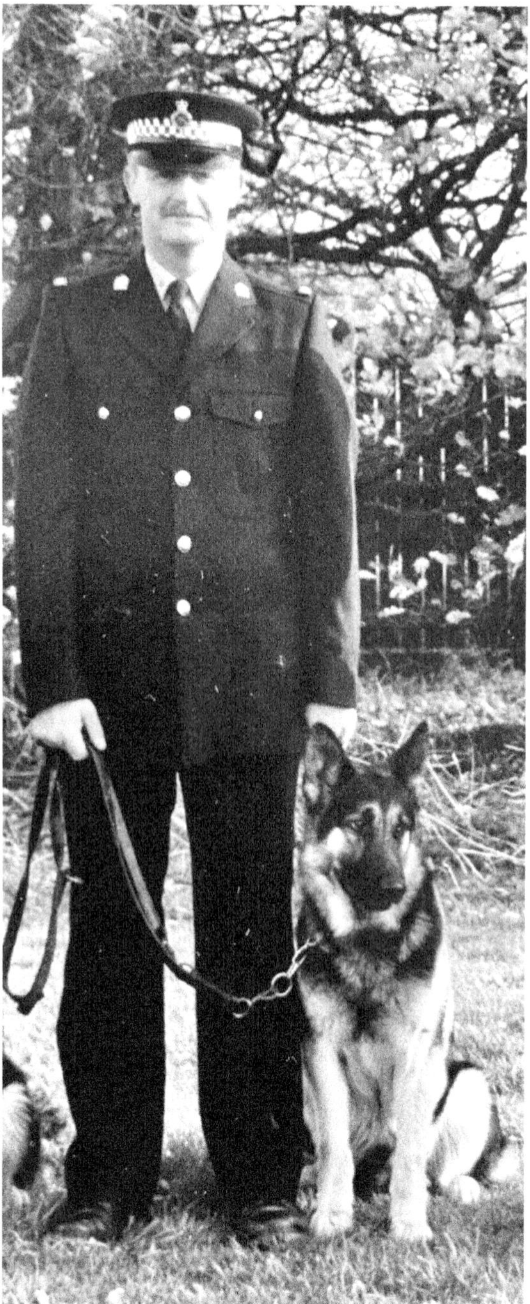

CONTENTS

PREFACE 1
CHAPTER 1 BACKGROUND 3
CHAPTER 2 POLICE CADETS 12
CHAPTER 3 POLICE CONSTABLE 1299 25
CHAPTER 4 FIRST POSTING 30
CHAPTER 5 SPECIALISATION 38
CHAPTER 6 SUITABILITY - YES OR NO? 40
CHAPTER 7 FIRST DOG – STORM 44
CHAPTER 8 POLICE DOG ZEUS 49
CHAPTER 9 WHERE DID IT ALL GO WRONG? 52
CHAPTER 10 BLUE 57
CHAPTER 11 MINERS' STRIKE 1984-1985 67
CHAPTER 12 ZAXON MOONRAKER 70
CHAPTER 13 INITIAL TRAINING (AGAIN) 74
CHAPTER 14 SERGEANT NEV AND THE POLICE DOG DISPLAY TEAM 79
CHAPTER 15 INSPECTOR MICK 87
CHAPTER 16 BITE FORCE 93
CHAPTER 17 GROUP 2 97
CHAPTER 18 X-RAY 99 116
CHAPTER 19 RETIREMENT 119
CHAPTER 20 LIFE AFTER ZAXON 122
THE FINAL CHAPTER 126

ABOUT THE AUTHOR

Mal is now contentedly retired and loves having time to spend with his wife, to whom he has been married for nearly half a century, exploring their favourite places, occasionally bird-watching. Since retiring, they have also gone on journeys around the world, visiting five different continents.

He enjoys watching sport, both live and on television, but his true passion lies in golf which he plays at least three times a week.

PREFACE

This project was originally meant to be a short story about my relationship with Zaxon Moonraker, my four-legged partner in the police force. As I continued to write, memories from my earlier life suddenly flooded back into my mind and the story morphed into an autobiographical document, leading up to when we started our relationship in 1986. It highlights the experiences and decisions which have helped shape me, from police cadet to policeman and, finally, dog handler.

I was born in Halifax in 1954 and then raised in Elland, a small West Yorkshire town between Halifax and Huddersfield, where I lived on council estates with my parents and younger sister and brother. My childhood was full of joy and the challenges it brings.

My early years consisted of both the positive and negative experiences common to everyone's life.

This account will hopefully give my future relatives a warts-and-all insight into my life.

Within the police force, I found my calling as a police dog handler. This specialised role required a unique set of skills and a deep connection with these exceptional canine companions. Trust, mutual respect and unwavering loyalty are the foundation of the bond between a handler and his canine partner.

The story describes the work I did with an exceptional dog who completely transformed my life and established a lifelong connection with me.

Our team was a formidable force, working together to apprehend the criminal fraternity and safeguard the public, but I will address that later.

CHAPTER ONE

BACKGROUND

During the 1950s and 1960s, I lived on a council estate with my parents, younger sister and brother. Our diligent parents set tight rules and boundaries for us, one of which was punctuality, which is a problem, if I'm honest, because I detest being late for anything and become upset with anyone who keeps me waiting. We were also taught proper etiquette, respect for others, and the importance of accepting responsibility for our own actions, discerning between right and wrong.

Mum worked in a woollen mill as a winder, warper, spinner and twister – not dancing routines, but all arduous tasks on heavy, noisy machinery. She began working full-time at the age of 14 and continued until she retired at the age of 64.

Dad was the fifth born of nine children, orphaned at the age of six. He started work as a labourer aged 14, gardening and building until working most of his life at a concrete manufacturer interspersed with two years of National Service, finally retiring aged 69. He would tell us about his difficult time in the orphanage as if he were a tragic Dickens character, yet it was clear that he had some fond memories of the experience he shared with his four brothers. I can't comprehend how they worked for so long in noisy, dirty and generally dreadful environments, but I greatly admire them for it.

The example Mum and Dad set in their work ethic had a big influence on me, yet I never wanted to follow their footsteps into manual labour, although I was hopeful that Dad's wicked sense of humour would be part of my DNA.

Money was tight, but we never went short. There was always food on the table and new clothes when needed, especially at Whitsuntide. We would wear our Sunday best for church and always had two holidays a year, usually on the east coast, in Bridlington or Scarborough, either in a rented caravan or, if money permitted, a boarding house. I must admit I enjoyed staying in caravans more as we could be louder and more boisterous in our play. I would hazard a guess that my parents preferred the boarding house in order to take a well-deserved rest from the demands of both work and home while raising three boisterous children.

Travelling to the east coast took well over three hours in those days, with no motorways to travel on, but we did it in style with my dad's pride and joy, a Royal Enfield 650cc motorcycle and sidecar. Both of them were leather-clad and helmeted, Dad riding, Mum on the pillion and the three of us squashed into the sidecar with luggage to last the week. What a sight that must have been.

After a few years, we upgraded to four wheels: a green and white Ford Consul MBN 744. We did have a three-wheeled

Reliant after the bike, but the less said about that the better.

It was in the MBN 744 that I had my first encounter with the police. Well, my dad did; I was just a bewildered backseat spectator taking in all the "action".

We were pulled over somewhere near York on our way to the east coast for a day out. My aunt and uncle were with us, so seven of us were wedged in the car like sardines!

During their brief conversation, the policeman informed Dad that he was driving at 33mph in a 30mph zone and warned him about the danger of speeding, especially as there were seven of us in the car. He was very polite with his scolding and ultimately let Dad off with a mild slap on the wrist. Dad gave a huge sigh of relief as, unbeknown to us, he only held a provisional driving licence which meant the copper missed out on a few traffic offences. We continued in an easterly direction at what felt like an excruciatingly slow snail's pace.

I fondly recall life being fun and I was always up to something. I delighted in playing sports with Dad, either football or cricket, in Saville Park, the expansive green parkland known as "the moor" in Halifax.

Dad and I were loyal Halifax Town fans since I was a tyke. Always battling at the foot of the league table, we would cheer them on no matter how badly they played, travelling across the country hoping for triumph. One particular escapade remains preserved in my mind: an FA Cup replay trip to Bristol City with two of my uncles. We regrettably stumbled to the ground 20 minutes after kick-off and were already two goals down. Despite our valiant efforts, we ended up losing 4-1, followed by a miserable six-hour journey back to Yorkshire. Despite having barely any sleep, I still got up early the next day for my paper round and then had to go to school! Even though I would've much preferred staying in bed all day, I didn't want to miss the thrilling football match I was playing later that afternoon.

When Dad was around, you knew there would be laughter and fun. He was a great comedian and prankster and had a unique ability to make us laugh. He also had an uncanny knack for embarrassing us, although I'm sure this was unintentional – sometimes!

One of those occasions was in a café in Bridlington. After ordering our food, he kept us engaged with his silly antics until it eventually arrived. When it did arrive, we could hardly believe our eyes! There seemed to be far less than ordered! Dad, not one to cause a fuss, decided to take matters into his own hands. He stood up on his chair and brought out his binoculars, peering at the tiny portions through the lenses. Everything else melted away as everyone broke out into fits of laughter – except for Mum and us three kids who had blushing cheeks from the embarrassment. Looking back now, it really was bloody hilarious.

School was a bit of a bore for me. From the age of 11, I attended Brooksbank Secondary Modern School in Elland. It had recently been a grammar school, so it was still academic, but sports were also high on the curriculum. I threw myself into all the sports on offer and very soon realised I wasn't going to be an academic. Most of the teachers were dull and mundane, but Mrs. Hinchcliffe turned my world upside down. She was a vision of beauty and my first crush, and I couldn't help but give in to my teenage impulse. History suddenly became my favourite subject, and although I wasn't learning much about historical facts, I was learning something about human pubescent biology.

I had no time for homework, and I must admit I did copy my maths from a girl in my class. That girl later became my wife, and not once in our 50 plus years together have we ever needed to use algebra or logarithms.

Needless to say, I didn't get any O' levels in these subjects although I am pretty good at mental arithmetic due to learning the times tables, parrot fashion, at junior school.

I enjoyed woodwork and technical drawing and achieved O' level grades in both. I was a member of all the school teams: football, cricket, volleyball, basketball, rugby union, athletics and cross country. I was also a decent tennis player and, at the age of 15, got through the first round at the Ilkley lawn tennis tournament for under 16s, only to lose in the second round to a posh kid donning a pristine monogrammed white shirt and shorts with at least half a dozen rackets and a yummy mummy applauding his every shot.

I represented Halifax schoolboys in football and basketball, giving me a great sense of pride.

I toiled from the age of 13 through to 16, delivering world and local news with three paper rounds. Every morning, Dad would wake me up at 5:30 a.m. sharp before setting off to work himself; I'd then leave right after him to start my strenuous round. In the evening and on Sunday mornings, I'd trudge through the streets, exhausted, until I finished off my deliveries with a smile on my face and a few quid in my pocket.

As I delivered the papers on an eerily empty street in Elland one morning, I detected my first crime. I saw someone I recognised riding a bike towards me. It was odd as the lad was from my school and it seemed too early for him to be out and about on a bike ride. Unless he was in training for the Tour de France, but seeing the plume of smoke as he took a drag on his cigarette, I very much doubted it.

He rode up to me as I delivered the newspapers and we began chatting. Something about the bike struck me – it looked exactly like my friend Depp's bike. When I mentioned it, the lad pedalled away into the dawn, leaving a trail of acrid smoke behind him.

The pieces clicked into place when I found out later that day that Depp's bike had been stolen during a burglary of their garage. The connection was clear, and I became certain that my shady biker had committed the burglary. My suspicions proved correct, and thanks to my sleuthing skills, Depp got his bike back.

Our parents were always supportive of our hobbies and interests, but never forced us to do anything we had no enthusiasm for.

I loved Dad coming to watch me play football, and a

massive lesson I learned from him was always to play fair. After one game, he gave me a bollocking for deliberately fouling an opponent, which was the first time I'd heard the phrase, "Cheating never wins." No matter what, he always praised me for any triumphs I had during a game.

When I was 15, I joined the school's old boys' team, my first taste of playing adult football. With the chance to play football on Saturday afternoons, I found myself playing for the school in the morning, followed by a game with the old boys and, for good measure, a Sunday morning team. If that wasn't enough exhaustion for one weekend, I also had to trudge around doing my three paper rounds! If I'd had a step counter back then, it would've been knackered trying to keep up.

During one old boys' match, I spun around to pass the ball back to the keeper but was met with an unexpected scene. There was my dad and Silas, the goalkeeper, hanging out by the goalpost, laughing and smoking a cigarette. I almost tripped over myself in shock and, sensing my confusion, Silas quickly put the fag between his lips before casually receiving my perfectly weighted left-footed back pass.

Mum was a quiet, hardworking woman and usually left it to Dad to tell us off when we needed it, yet we knew we'd done something wrong by a certain look she would give us.

She would always tend to my cuts and grazes, of which there were many due to my playing sports, all done with care and love. You can't beat a knob of butter rubbed on a lump after a bang on the head or the sting of TCP applied to an open cut or graze. Now, I'm no medic, but vinegar and brown paper may have been a better alternative to butter!

What I remember most about my boyhood was always laughing and having fun. Dad was also a maestro on the mouth organ and we would often accompany him during family sing-songs, something I have fond memories of.

At 15, trying to decide what I was going to do for the rest of my life was difficult. I knew the grades forecast for me wouldn't allow me to forge a career in astrophysics, brain surgery, or similar mundane jobs.

I attended a careers convention at school, checking out various displays and jobs on offer. I could have used my skills in woodwork or technical drawing, but they didn't overly excite me. I would have liked to have been a professional footballer, but I didn't quite make the grade despite thinking I was the next Bobby Charlton. I'm sure I would have been a good sports teacher, but again, I needed some academic qualifications to achieve that.

I then came across a display that would eventually fashion my adult life. "Join the police cadets" the sign said, so I sat down with a policeman, who told me all the virtues of policing; well, maybe not all.

In those days, there was no need for a degree – you just had to pass an entrance exam. Plus, there was the opportunity to play sports in the cadets. It all sounded glamorous, so I applied to join and passed the entrance exam. I also had an interview, as did my parents, who were also background checked. It was a relief that they didn't learn about Dad driving on a provisional licence with no L-plates or insurance.

We were obviously deemed to have the correct moral fibre and I was successful in everything that was required. So, on 7th September 1970, I became Police Cadet 22 Nutbrown, earning a whopping pre-decimal 8 pounds, 8 shillings and 0 pence.

Also in 1970, on reaching the age of 16, I became the proud owner of a Lambretta LI 150cc motor scooter, which my dad taught me to ride. On my first outing, in a yard where he worked, he taught me all about the clutch, gears, brakes and accelerator. Unfortunately, he didn't teach me how not to fall off, which I did with panache, my arse receiving a gravel rash. I re-mounted and soon got the hang of riding it until a woman driving out of a side street in Brighouse knocked me off, denting my pride as well as my highly polished side panel.

I had another encounter with the police when they stopped me while I was giving Dad a lift home from work. I was displaying L-plates, but Dad, a full motorcycle licence holder, was allowed to tutor me – another experience with a polite policeman.

I had the scooter until I was 18, when I sadly had to sell it to buy an engagement ring for my maths-minded girlfriend. I wanted fifty pounds for it, but the buyer only offered forty, mathematically speaking only eighty per cent of what I'd hoped for. With a heavy heart, I accepted the offer and bought a white gold solitaire diamond ring. Only time would tell if it was a wise investment but oh, I did miss my scooter.

CHAPTER TWO

POLICE CADETS

Year one: 7th September 1970

I rode my red and white charger, wearing a matching helmet, into Bishopgarth, the West Yorkshire police training school in Wakefield, to start my training. Fear began to creep in and, once I'd dismounted, it was discipline followed by more discipline. The first two weeks of induction were dedicated to fitness and drill exercises, and, despite my assumption that I was in decent physical shape, fuck me, the PE classes nearly killed me. My body was in pain, aching uncomfortably until it eventually adjusted to the intensity of the exercises.

The Chief Inspector in charge of cadet training was an incredibly nice chap called Stanley who welcomed us into the cadet service with his softly spoken tone. During that time, I was quite proficient at imitating voices, particularly Stanley's. On more than one occasion, cadets stood to attention for him without realizing that it was me speaking in his voice while hiding from their sight, looking bemused when Stanley wasn't there.

On the first session of drill, we met Sergeant Ralph, a big, burly man with a large ginger handlebar moustache. He was intimidatingly loud and carried a silver-topped swagger stick under his arm. His uniform was pristine and he had the shiniest boots I'd ever seen. He shouted orders at everyone, sometimes with great one-liners. "Your eyes look like a kingfisher's arsehole!" he screamed at one girl cadet who was wearing too much eye makeup.

"Attention, stand at ease, quick march, left, right, left, right!" I heard those commands every day and even in my dreams for a few weeks. Eventually, I started to enjoy the drill, and it taught me the importance of teamwork and pride in my appearance and demeanour. Sadly, drill is no longer a common practice in modern police training.

We were taught the art of pressing our uniforms and bulling our boots, creating a highly polished toecap. Using a duster to build up layers of 'spit and polish' in small circular motions with Kiwi polish, "Not fucking Cherry Blossom!" which was screamed on the parade square many times. Anybody who has bulled a pair of boots will tell you a highly polished toecap is a thing of beauty. All this discipline may nowadays be seen as bullying, but I never felt that at the time. As well as teaching me respect for my team and pride in my appearance, it also taught me self-discipline.

Not everyone on the training staff was pleasant; there was a diminutive Scotsman who acted like putting us through pain and suffering was his only goal in life. He was an amateur boxer and made us all put on a pair of gloves for a two-minute bout, fully absorbed in laughing at anyone who got smacked in the face or knocked on their arse.

On day one, all the male cadets were told to get a haircut whether they needed it or not. Over the next few days, we all trudged to Joe the Pole's barber shop in Wakefield where I got a 'short back and sides', shorter than I'd ever had before. Joe must have made quite a bit of cash with all the unwilling cadet customers, and I often wondered if he trimmed Ralph's moustache into its magnificent shape.

After two weeks of physical torture, we were thrown into Wakefield Technical College. PC Plod had never mentioned this during the careers convention, and now I learned I was expected to study for more O' levels – English and Sociology, of all things. I had already failed English once and didn't know what Sociology was, and I still have no idea if I'm honest. Yet somehow, despite all the odds, I passed both exams! Was I secretly turning into an academic? Definitely not; now, where was that sport they promised me?

It's funny the things that stick with you over time. I remember attending lessons on 'the art of public speaking' with the tutor, Charles Moston-Hughes, and although the lessons didn't come with a certificate or qualification, they must have helped in some small way, giving me the courage to stand up in front of people, giving talks and presenting lectures when I later became a police dog training instructor.

The cadet training staff taught us basic law and other police-related subjects, as well as continuing drill and physical education including swimming. On one visit to the pool, we were all made to climb to the highest board, which at the top appeared to be, shall we say, 'a fucking long way down'.

Sitting on the edge, curled up like a ball waiting for the command to go before rolling off, staying in the curled position until hitting the water at Mach 10. One cadet refused the order to take off so we all had to watch and wait for about 20 minutes until, with our encouragement, he rolled forward, letting out a blood-curdling scream on the way down whilst performing a double pike with a one and a half twist before belly flopping into the water with a loud slap.

We were sectioned off into groups and began playing sports. Sergeant Major Ralph established a football tournament between all the groups, with seven games in total. I won a prize for my performance as the top scorer, netting 14 goals. My reward from Ralph was not a fucking tin of Cherry Blossom polish but the far superior Kiwi, a clothes brush, boot brushes and duster. He was also responsible for managing the cadets football team, of which I was a member. He was an avid Leeds United fan, so the training we had came right out of Don Revie's coaching manual, missing out the chapters on kicking people up in the air and cheating!

I look back fondly on the day we travelled to Glasgow to compete in the semi-final of the National Cadets Cup. On our first night there, we had a memorable visit to Parkhead, the home of Celtic Football Club, where we saw the European cup, Celtic being the first British champions of Europe in 1967.

I had one shining moment in the game, when I scored a goal, but it wasn't enough as we lost 3-2. But hey, that's football, and at least we had a good night out! Most of us got quite pissed, and when I woke up the following morning, my pristine light-blue suit was as wrinkled as a baboon's arse when I climbed out of bed still wearing it.

Each police division had its own highly spirited football team playing in a league where the tackles were not always within the rules of the game.

I quickly learned that police sports could be quite 'intense', with some real thugs knocking us young cadets around – when they could catch us! But it was all good fun, and I learned to take it on the chin, using my superior skill to evade the dirty bastards.

Regrettably, I was unable to attend our grand passing-out parade despite a year of strenuous training. During that time, I worked tirelessly towards the parade and PE display, but fate had other plans for me: an unexpected emergency led to me undergoing an operation to remove a burst appendix. Despite my absence, Sergeant Ralph extended an invitation to my parents to attend. They were thrilled to be there, taking pride in all the work I had put in leading up to it. During the ceremony, they were presented with my football trophy and boot brush prize, which they later delivered to me in my hospital bed.

Year 2: HQ

My second year of training was spent working in various departments at the force headquarters in Wakefield.

For three months, I worked in Force Control, answering

motorway emergency telephones, employing my best telephone etiquette to converse with members of the public, some of whom were dim-witted, arrogant, or just plain rude. I took reports of road accidents, breakdowns and other road-related incidents before passing the details onto the radio operators so they could dispatch the road traffic units. I would also have to organise rescues for broken-down vehicles by contacting the AA, RAC, or other breakdown services. Despite being noisy with the constant hum of voices and crackling radio messages, it was a nice working environment where I learned a lot about the relationship between the radio operators and officers on the front line, and I thoroughly enjoyed my three months working there.

My next posting was in the HQ mail room, where, basically, I was the Chief Constable's personal servant. It was run by a civilian who would now definitely be considered a bully. He was known as Rag-Arm due to the fact he only had one arm. He had a fearsome reputation for making cadets run errands, not only for the chief but other senior officers, some of whom thought they were gods. Parading smugly around HQ, they wouldn't acknowledge us cadets, dismissing us without making eye contact or even a nod in our direction. Despite being underage, I was often ordered to nip downtown to buy fags and booze for them. My mind fantasising as to what the higher ranks were getting up to in their ivory tower. Rag-arm would deliver the goodies to them himself, I'm sure making out it was him who'd trudged to the shops in the pissing rain.

It was the worst three months I spent as a cadet, with Rag-Arm bollocking us for even a minute mistake, such as putting the mail in the wrong box or even having a laugh, which, unbeknown to him, was usually at his expense.

My final posting was in the Fingerprint Department, and although I quickly became acquainted with arches, loops and whorls, my main task was much more important: making tea twice a day. That's fifty cups a day, five days per week for ten weeks, an amazing total of 2,500 steaming mugs of strong Yorkshire tea. The smoke in this large room seemed to thicken during our tea breaks when loud laughter mingled with police banter and relentless teasing of the young cadets. It was a friendly, smoky atmosphere that I will never forget.

One of the pranksters gave me a requisition form to take to the stores requesting some white fingerprint ink. When I questioned its use, he stated that they used it when taking fingerprints of black people, which at the time seemed logical. Once when I visited the stores I saw another cadet who had been sent for some elbow grease and a long stand …

During this second year, I lived in lodgings with two other cadets. Although we got on well and had plenty of laughs, the landlady was an old battle-axe who made it clear that she would report us for being late or any misbehaviour to PC Geoff, the new PTI who had taken the place of the wee boxing Scotsman. We had a curfew of 10:30 p.m. unless there was a cadet dance at the police sports ground two miles away, when the time was extended until midnight. On one occasion after a dance, I raced back home, arriving breathless, just seconds before midnight, to avoid a report to PC Geoff, who was also Ralph's deputy and trainer of the cadets' football team.

Although the year wasn't easy, I made a lot of friends and had enjoyable times socialising with them, usually in pubs. The Grove, a pub on the edge of the city centre, was our favourite spot to hang out until the cadet training staff raided it, kicking out all the underage cadets. I had recently turned 18, so I was allowed to finish my pint with a couple of other adults!

Nevertheless, we were all punished for it the next day, being called in for extra PE, drill and more pain.

Year 3: Divisional training

Finally, the year was finished, and I was transferred to the Halifax division, my great hometown! I had the pleasure of living with my parents again ... probably much to their surprise.

My year at the division spanned various departments, including prosecutions, collators office and CID administration, where my future father-in-law, PC Price, worked too. My meal breaks were spent refining my snooker skills; there was a table in the station and the CID admin sergeant was a force snooker champion. We'd challenge each other to frames of snooker during our breaks, and this paid off when I won the Force Championship in 1986. Then, I went on to win several pairs championships with my friend Craig, until we eventually claimed the National Pairs Snooker

Championship in 1997 by defeating teams from all over Great Britain. Apart from snooker, most of my day was taken up with mundane office duties such as filing and answering phones.

I took a special interest in road traffic policing after a one-month attachment. I particularly enjoyed speeding to emergencies, the blue lights and sirens sending adrenaline coursing through my veins. It was my first foray into actual police work and interacting with the public. I also attended a five-week intensive driving course in Wakefield, after which I passed my driving test. Throughout my service, I always prided myself on my competence behind the wheel, adhering to the police system of driving.

The last three months of my cadet tenure were spent beat training in the town centre. With that experience, I was able to learn what it meant to be a real-life police constable, and I loved it so much that I wanted to stay with the same team in Halifax when I became a PC, but unfortunately things didn't work out that way. The shift had some great characters, namely Sergeant Keith, with whom I crossed paths several times over the course of my service, becoming firm friends, and even now, after fifty years, we still play golf together.

But the most exciting part was when I got to drive my first police car – an uncomfortable minivan, though at the time it felt like I was driving a Rolls Royce.

Cadets weren't supposed to work after 10 p.m., but I was sanctioned to work the 5 p.m. until 1 a.m. shift. This is when I really started to learn about the ugly side of the great British public. Drunken idiots fighting, violence, people being sick and pissing everywhere. My partner for one shift, Joe, arrested a man who was shamelessly pissing through some railings at the side of the post office. This was in broad daylight and in full view of the public. Exciting stuff! My first ever arrest was an open-air pisser locked up for being drunk and disorderly; he started shouting and swearing as we interrupted him mid-flow. He was bailed and never turned up in court, so the magistrates issued an arrest warrant. Joe offered a reward of a pint for anybody on the shift who executed the warrant. I'm not sure whether anybody claimed that pint.

Whilst patrolling in the transit van, we responded to some youths causing trouble at the Royal Infirmary. When we arrived, one of them ran off. I chased him down a side street, outpacing two of our more seasoned officers. I finally caught up to him and brought him to the ground. One of the "Bobbies" came over and gave him a slap as punishment for trying to run away, and my old pal Joe followed up with another slap. This was lesson one: if you run away, you'll get slapped if you're caught; hopefully this would prevent them from running away in the future.

Upon investigation, nothing serious had happened because they were just horsing around and annoying the staff. So we drove them out onto the moors where they were left to find their own way home. Though this might not be allowed these days, this is what the "Ways and Means Act" considered acceptable.

Sometimes, after the late shift, I would go to the Acca, a well-known Halifax nightclub, with some of the lads for a couple of pints, another facet of police life: socialisation!

Outward bound courses

Once a year we endured a gruelling three weeks of outdoor activities in the picturesque Yorkshire Dales. We were pushed to our limits; hiking, canoeing, reading maps, rock climbing, each day full of exciting but arduous tasks. It all sounds great, but with only four hours of sleep a night, it started taking its toll on us mentally and physically.

Some of the instructors loved to rouse us out of our slumber, using things like banging pots and pans or sounding the fire rattle. They even went as far as starting a "fire" in a bucket, tossing wet leaves into it to create plenty of smoke and confusion; we were convinced we were about to confront an actual inferno! After herding us all outside, bewildered and exhausted, they would force us to do another PE session or other physical challenge, much to our irritation, before letting us back into the warmth of our beds. Just when we thought we could finally rest, they would pull yet another stunt to arouse us from our a much-needed kip.

We had to keep our tongues in check to avoid paying into the dreaded swear box. Some of the instructors took delight in catching us when we least expected it. Lurking around corners or hiding behind walls, surprising us with massive grins on hearing a filthy faux-pas.

A friend of mine was told he owed 20 pence. He said, "Make it 25 and fuck off."

Certain cadets were known for their unsavoury language, resulting in hefty fines, but not me as the bastards never fucking caught me so it cost me fuck all.

During my time as a cadet, I survived three outward-bound courses, and although I didn't enjoy them at the time, looking back, they were certainly character-building experiences as well as great fun, bonding and laughing with other cadets, and the lack of sleep and pain was soon forgotten. It also served to build up not only stamina but resilience, advantageous for a police officer.

After almost three years as a cadet, I looked back fondly on most of the experiences. I enjoyed the marching and, perversely, the bullshit, all of it turning us boys and girls into men very quickly. I met some amazing people, some not so, but it gave me an invaluable insight into different kinds of characters, providing me with lots of connections and contacts for when I became a police officer.

I made some fantastic friends during my time in the cadets, and I'm still in touch with a few of them today. I started out as a shy, immature boy, but by the end of my three years, I had become a man (though some might say still immature).

After passing my driving test, I bought a Morris 1000 motor car, TCP 661. It may have been a shitty brown colour, scratched and dented all over with a rotting floor, but it was mine and cost me only £55. It was certainly no racing car, taking about half an hour to get from 0 to 40 mph, but I still loved it. I and my maths brainiac girlfriend went everywhere in that car, even a trip to South Wales to visit her relatives, only breaking down once due to overheating.

CHAPTER THREE

POLICE CONSTABLE 1299

My journey as a fully fledged policeman began on the day of my 19th birthday in 1973, with a ten-week course at the prestigious Police Training School in Pannal Ash, near Harrogate. It was attended by recruits from many forces, not just West Yorkshire.

I'm sure the politically correct police of today are cringing at my admission, but I was a policeman and damn proud of it! My preferred pronouns are strictly he/him/his, not they/them/their, zie/zim/zies, or any other non-binary creation. I liked driving to jobs with the lights and sirens blaring, so perhaps I should have identified as a "traffic person" with the pronouns wee/wa/woo/wa. But that's enough ranting for now, although I can't promise there won't be more later in this tale.

For the first week, we were transported by the force bus, so we all arrived together. The training was from Monday to Friday, with weekends off, which I spent at home, but the following nine weeks I drove myself there on a Sunday night, making sure I was ready for action the following morning.

We were accommodated in a dormitory with around a

dozen people, each with their own bed space, which had to be kept spotless. Every morning, we'd fold our sheets and blankets according to specific measurements and stack them on the lower edge of the bed. If not positioned or measured correctly, the "bed-pack" would be left strewn across the floor when we arrived back after lessons – all very military. I still remember the symphony of snores, burps and farts echoing throughout the dorm like a badly tuned orchestra, giving the place its own distinctive stale odour.

Former cadets had an advantage on the course because we were already well versed in drill, discipline, boot bulling and, of course, bull shit, all of which we practised from day one.

During one of our marching sessions, Alex, the drill sergeant, made the policewoman next to me cry. When stamping our feet, we had to really bang them down, making a loud, synchronised noise. He stood eyeball to eyeball with her and shouted in his thick Glaswegian accent, "I could make more noise banging my fucking penis against that flagpole." It was hard not to laugh out loud, especially for the teary-eyed Pee Wee, which I know sounds a derogatory term, but I can assure you it was not as inappropriate as some of the things I heard to describe policewomen.

Lessons in criminal and traffic law were done mainly in the classroom but then acted out in practical situations. We were also expected to pass fitness, self-defence and first-aid tests, and gain at least the bronze medallion lifesaving award in the swimming pool. Although I wasn't a strong swimmer, I was adequate at swimming in my pyjamas and diving for a brick, something else I hoped I would never need to use in my career. Walking to the swimming pool or around the site for practical exercises was all done in a march, maintaining professional teamwork.

Self-defence was some Japanese martial art, empty-hand skills, and also the correct use of your wooden truncheon. If used, this had to be struck across the violent criminal's bony joints of their body: shoulders, elbows and knees. I can tell you now that it doesn't work, especially if the criminal is pissed, high on LSD or other illegal substances.

Menial duties were also on the agenda: guarding the front gate, patrolling the grounds and buildings, even serving behind the bar of the pub, pulling pints or warming and selling the pies. One night every week we played bingo, and unless you were on menial duty, you were expected to turn up. It was a great night, although by the end of the course everybody knew the bingo callers' one-liners for each number, so the laughs became fewer. There was the usual "2 little ducks, 22" to which everybody replied "Quack 2-3, quack" or "2 fat ladies, 88" with a reply of "Ooph 2-3, ooph", and then there were a few inappropriate ones like "6 and 9 upside down 69." I can't continue with the sexual innuendo reply to that number, but it never failed to get a laugh.

We also played sports, and, as the course took place during May, June and July, it was athletics and cricket on offer. I played one game of cricket for the Pannal Ash team along with some other students and instructors, and also represented our class in athletics, running in the 200 yards.

Not a fucking chance; a couple of the runners had brought their own starting blocks, wore spikes, and were at least 30 yards down the track before I got into my stride in my Tesco tearaway trainers.

It was a tough and, in many ways, very intense course. There were times when we were all pushed to our limits, but we got through it and, in the end, passed out as police constables, becoming a tight-knit unit, forming memories that would last forever.

Fortunately, I'd already lost my appendix, so I was able to attend the final graduation parade. Mum, Dad and my maths guru – now fiancée, wearing a sparkling solitaire ring – came to watch the glorious spectacle.

It started with a drill display performed to music: the Scottish drill pig's favourite bagpipe band and also John Philip Sousa's The Liberty Bell March, which was the theme tune for *Monty Python's Flying Circus*, a popular television comedy at the time. I don't think I have ever felt as proud, either as an individual or as part of a team. I also took part in the self-defence exhibition, Japanese empty-hand skills, but not displaying the correct use of my truncheon.

After all the action, we had tea and sandwiches with our guests, followed by lots of emotional moments and tears. Not me; I just had something in my eye when we said our goodbyes. It was a great day to end a brilliant course with some fantastic people, including our class instructors Fred and Dave, who treated us like grown-ups, as did most of the instructors, one of whom was an inspector whom I mimicked quite well. Towards the end of the course, he came into our lesson, and we all showed respect for his rank by standing up but this time, he didn't shout out his usual instruction to sit down. He just looked straight at me and intimated that I should say it, in his voice. I gulped, taking a deep breath before shouting in his loud accent: "Right, sit down!" I thought I was going to get a bollocking, but he just laughed, saying it was the best he'd ever heard before walking out.

CHAPTER FOUR

FIRST POSTING

On completion of my training, I was less than thrilled to have been posted to the Huddersfield division rather than my hometown of Halifax. Despite this temporary setback, I was fortunate to be allowed to stay with my parents until I got married in 1974 to the woman who had saved me from mathematics tedium! After saying our vows, we moved into a police house within the division that we were able to live in free of charge.

In 1975, our first child, a daughter, was born, and the following year we moved into another rent-free police house in a much quieter upmarket area.

My role as a "Bobby" consisted of pounding the streets on foot, sometimes in the response car, or even driving the "Black Maria" as it was still called, despite it being light blue. This was only used on Friday and Saturday nights, flying around the usual rough pubs and clubs, dealing with fights, assaults, stabbings, and arresting drunken idiots, booking them in at the station, only to repeat until after 2 am when all the clubs had shut and the rest of the halfwits fucked off home.

Driving the Black Maria was an exhilarating experience:

always on the go, dashing around the division, responding to a myriad of fascinating incidents. One crazy occasion that we raced to stands out: we received a report of a half-naked man going berserk, crazily smashing windows by lunging through them into people's living rooms. Just imagine the scenario: you're calmly enjoying a cup of cocoa while watching *The Incredible Hulk* on Friday night TV, only to have a half-naked man burst through your window, shattering the peace as well as the double glazing.

As we arrived, "the Hulk", wearing only a torn shirt, dramatically leapt from a high wall, landing arse first on the roof of a car before violently crashing onto the pavement with a deafening thud. Our immediate reaction was to swiftly approach and apprehend him, which proved difficult due to his half-naked and blood-soaked state, a result of some severe cuts. The struggle intensified, requiring the collaborative efforts of at least six of us to subdue him. Eventually, we managed to bring him under control and promptly secured him using handcuffs. Not stopping there, we employed a dog handler's lead to bind his legs, ensuring he remained restrained throughout the journey to the hospital. It transpired he was high on LSD and this was when I realised a truncheon strike to the joints has no effect. As we escorted him, our uniforms served as a visual testimony to the chaotic confrontation, bearing the unmistakable marks of the relentless struggle.

I had started the shift at 2 pm on Friday, working with hardly a break until 6 am on Saturday, only for me to realise I had to return for my next shift at 2 pm. On my return, I was absolutely knackered as I embarked on yet another hectic 16-hour Saturday night shift.

At the time, there were a lot of outdated bylaws giving police officers power of arrest. The Huddersfield Improvement Act of the 1870s had a clause allowing constables to order people out of town – or face the consequences. This was useful when individuals became argumentative but not quite disorderly enough for an arrest. You just had to give them a warning to leave, or they could be arrested for "failing to move on", be given a night in the cells, incurring a hefty fine of £2, which must have been a fortune back in the 1870s. Even in the 1970s, it was still a lot; a pint of beer at the police station bar only cost 15 pence, so £2 = 13.3 pints.

I vividly recall a particular night when I overheard on my radio a fellow officer in pursuit of a troublemaker who happened to be heading towards my beat. Reacting promptly, I intercepted the individual and handed him over to my weary colleague. Curious about the reason for his arrest, I was astonished to hear him say it was for "failing to move on".

"Failing to move on? He's fucking running away from you!" I retorted. This led to a necessary change in the charge, ultimately resulting in an offence for disorderly conduct, and consequently, a rather weighty fine of 13.3 pints.

Most of my role as a town centre beat officer entailed walking the streets, proudly standing tall – at least 6 feet 4 inches in my helmet – in a well-pressed uniform and highly polished boots, giving me a sense of control. I encountered lost-and-found items, and children, shoplifters, reckless drivers; I guided elderly people across the street, and even told the time. Point duty was one of my favourite tasks as it made me feel powerful when directing traffic. We also had to manage more serious crimes like burglaries, robberies and various violent incidents.

The first time I was confronted with death occurred in the early morning, an hour into my shift. A man in his early thirties had chosen to take his life by hanging himself from a tree in Greenhead Park. When I received the call about someone being seen hanging around in the park, I had no idea it would end up being so solemn. Now whenever I walk through the same park, the horrific image of that day replays in my head.

Shortly after the grim discovery, an inspector paid me a visit at the mortuary. Surprisingly, he entered singing the tune "While swinging in the park one day," offering a glimpse of the gallows humour that helps police officers cope with these distressing situations. As peculiar as it may sound, "the gallows humour" was not intended as a deliberate pun.

Not long into my career, I was given the opportunity to mentor new officers. As a tutor constable, it was my duty to teach new officers how to become successful policemen and policewomen on the beat. Although I was fairly inexperienced myself, thankfully I was able to do so successfully and even made lasting friendships with some of those whom I mentored.

I encountered sights, sounds and smells that have etched themselves permanently into my mind, defying any attempt to eradicate them from my memory. Even to this day, these memories still emerge, uninvited and involuntary.

I think people felt reassured seeing police officers patrolling the streets, a sight that is all but gone. It's not an indictment of current police officers but rather an observation of how standards have dropped due to politically correct management and governments of all political persuasions. I may be considered a dinosaur, but I look at all the antisocial activities, muggings and stabbings occurring throughout every day, not just at weekends amongst drunken hooligans. Things are becoming more violent as gangs fight over turf or drugs, not averse to using knives or guns, and insufficient police numbers to deal with it all.

Plodding around the streets at night was a different story.

When our shift began, we were assigned a small area of town to patrol. We weren't allowed to stray from our beat; we'd be in trouble if caught by our sergeant or inspector, who would admonish us by making a scathing remark in our pocketbook, highlighted in red pen. But sometimes we took the risk of having a smoke and chatting with a colleague down one of the many yards, out of sight. A bigger risk was slipping into one of the local pubs after hours. I mean, I heard rumours about some officers doing that and grabbing a pint (or two), but it's not something I ever did!

I was caught red-handed by a sergeant, away from my

assigned beat with two of my fellow officers. We were lugging around a mannequin we had found and claimed to be taking it to the lost property office. In reality, we were headed to another officer's beat so we could hang it up for him to find in one of the dark alleys, a prank to pass the time during our shift.

We had already had some fun with the dummy before being snagged by the sarge.

One of my colleagues removed the head, putting his helmet on it, then buttoned his coat above his head, carrying the helmeted head under his arm. We were in fits of laughter when a drunk stumbled along the road, and our metaphysical figure appeared in front of him, emerging slowly from out of a dark eerie yard. The guy was stunned, staring in disbelief as he watched the apparition vanish back into the yard before staggering away down the street himself. It's funny to think about whether he ever told anyone about his encounter with "PC 3951", the ghost of six beat.

When we weren't smoking, laughing or taking the piss out of each other, we would inspect the properties on our beat. We had to make sure everything was secure before and after meal breaks. If we missed an unlocked premises or a burglary occurred during our shift, we could expect an earful and be called out of bed in the morning to explain why we had missed it. Thankfully, this never happened to me, but I know of some who were not so lucky.

At 5 a.m., everyone left their beat to go get coffee at a local hotel. This was a chance for us to catch up and talk about the shift, any dickheads we'd dealt with, but mainly just to have a laugh. Most of the sergeants and inspectors knew we went there, some even joining us, although there were a few sticklers who would try to catch us off guard, if they could catch us at all. Luckily, we all knew who they were and had methods of avoiding them, which gave us a good feeling when successful. Some mornings, a certain sergeant used to park his own car in the railway station car park overlooking the hotel in the hope of catching us out; he didn't seem to realise he could only see the front door, so it was easy for us to escape through the back and make our way to the station using the back streets and yards, and climbing walls we knew like the backs of our hands.

I had great experiences on the beat with some wonderful colleagues and eccentric characters.

One of my favourite eccentrics was Sergeant Geoff, nicknamed Barney Rubble due to his similarity to the cartoon character in both appearance and voice. He wasn't far from retirement and was a decorated veteran of World War Two. He was straight talking, with a dry sense of humour, and didn't take any shit from anybody. One late evening, I was the designated driver of a Panda car when Barney decided to accompany me. I stopped the car at a road junction and looked to my right where I saw a group of four youths, one of whom was damaging a car by jumping on the bonnet. I immediately set off towards them like a formula one driver on steroids. The lads scattered, running in different directions, and went briefly out of sight until one of them reappeared. I was driving alongside him when Barney shouted, "Run the bastard, run him!"

Taking this to mean "run him down", I gently clipped him with the front near-side wing, momentarily causing him to lose balance. As he was landing on his feet, Barney opened his door, crashing it into the fleeing hooligan and knocking him to the ground. It was at this stage I realised he wasn't the kid who'd jumped on the car bonnet but one of his mates. He was arrested on suspicion of causing damage and handed over to some other officers while Barney and I went searching for the one who had actually committed the crime. Around half a mile from the scene, I identified him walking casually along the street so we stopped, collared him and, as was customary, I went to give him a slap for running away. I was surprised as Barney stopped me from doing so, calmly placing the youth in the car before he gave him a slap across his head. "Never do it where t'public can see thee," he stated in his gruff Yorkshire twang, teaching a young officer a valuable lesson.

My time working on the beat sometimes felt like a never-ending struggle of blood, sweat and tears. Despite the moments of laughter and fun that I clung to, there were darker things that I wished to forget, yet these moments were instrumental in forging the man I became, and every single lesson learned during this time was invaluable for the rest of my service.

CHAPTER FIVE

SPECIALISATION

During the two years of my probationary period, I spent a number of weeks in various departments such as Road Traffic and CID, giving me options for specialisation further down the line. Neither really appealed much, but I found myself leaning more towards Road Traffic because I was good at dealing with traffic offences and road accidents, and I enjoyed the fast-paced siren calls (blue and twos).

While I'd never been particularly drawn to the dog section, I was fortunate enough to work alongside a couple of dog handlers who actually got their dogs out at incidents. At that time, a lot didn't; they made excuses not to. It was either too hot or cold, too wet or too dry, or some other flimsy excuse. Quite often, we would hear the phrase, "Nowt here for me, kid." In fact, the dog section didn't really have a good reputation, with many often seen as work-shy, scruffy policemen only getting the dog out for a piss or shit.

After two years of service, we had to attend a two-week continuation course during which we were all asked how we would like to specialise in the future. Almost everyone said Road Traffic, CID, some even choosing to remain as a beat Bobby. When I said dog handler, the smug instructor said in the smarmiest of tones, "There's always one."

"What a fucking wanker," I thought.

Despite him later being promoted to inspector, working in Huddersfield, my opinion of him never changed!

Unlike Sergeant Smarmy, the two dog handlers were always on the lookout for thieves, villains and vagabonds. They inspired me, and I sometimes helped out with their training; I would hide for the dogs to find me and even wear a protective sleeve so they could practise biting criminals. After four years of being a plod, I decided that I wanted to find out if I was suited to be a dog handler and if the role was suited to me. My other goal was to ram Sergeant Smarmy's words down his fucking throat.

I submitted an application to attend a dog handler suitability course to determine if I would be a good fit.

Despite my sergeant signing the application right away, my inspector called me into his office. He mentioned that he had high regard for me as a policeman and tutor and did not want me to waste my career as a dog handler. His poor opinion of the dog section only made me more curious and determined.

After a few months, it was decided that I would attend a course in November 1977, and I was determined that if I passed, I would be the type of handler who actually worked the dog for its true purpose: catching villains and protecting the public.

CHAPTER SIX

SUITABILITY - YES OR NO?

When November 1977 rolled around, I set off to Wakefield, the police dog training school, for a two-week Police Dog Handling Suitability Course. At the end of the long driveway, I came across a large property comprising four large, red-brick, impressive buildings which encircled a large field with woods and fields extending beyond. One of the wooded areas was fenced off. I later discovered it was nicknamed Shit Alley for reasons that would soon become clear. The kennels were housed in the back of one of the buildings, while four others overlooked the spacious field.

I had just stepped out of my car to a cacophony of barking dogs when a hefty man wearing overalls with an unmistakable ruddy face came close. I remembered him from the Huddersfield division where he was a dog handler with an invisible dog.

He now worked at the training school and lived in one of the red brick buildings nearby. He asked, in his thick Geordie accent, if I had arrived to take the suitability course, and when I said yes, he cautioned me: "Better take off your coat and gloves, pet. Roy will think you're a softie."

I didn't dare to argue, even though I knew that I was being a softie – it was freezing! A few moments later, I met Roy, a tall man sporting a silver-grey moustache with a trilby hat covering his balding head. I also met Clive, who was also there to assess his suitability to be a dog handler.

Initially, we were given a tour of the kennels and told our expected duties for the next two weeks. Cleaning up shit and scrubbing kennels were all part of the experience. Several metal buckets and shovels were strategically placed around the field and Shit Alley for handlers to put their dog's shit into. Part of our job was to collect these buckets at the end of the day, empty them into the sluice, replenish them with disinfectant, and replace them for the next day's load. The sight and stench of dog shit mixed with toxic disinfectant will haunt my nasal passages forever.

Following lunch, we were each assigned a dog for the next two weeks. Roy showed us how to groom them, which we had to do each morning. We then received instructions on how to enter the kennel, making sure the dog couldn't run out, and the correct way to attach a lead and metal choke chain collar before exiting safely with our new furry friend.

I cautiously approached the kennel, and was greeted by a loud bark from a good-looking, black and gold German Shepherd called Rex. I wasn't sure if he was aggressively telling me to fuck off or just barking excitedly saying hello. I tried to remain calm, but it wasn't easy with Rex jumping up and down with excitement. I didn't want him to pick up on any apprehension, so I tried to look as confident as possible when I entered his kennel. It was a sight to behold; Rex bounced around like a rubber ball while I tried not to look like a complete clown as I attempted to put on his lead and collar. After much effort, I finally managed to open the door. Rex dragged me out immediately, almost knocking me over in the process. Geordie and a few others were watching as if they had been waiting for this exact moment, looking for some laughs at my expense as I tripped over the frame, nearly ending up on my arse.

I had a fantastic two weeks, full of new experiences and fun. We took the dogs for walks, received lectures on all aspects of police dog training, shovelled shit, laid scent for the dogs to track, shovelled shit, and played criminals for the trained pooches to locate, bark at, and bite; did I mention the shit shovelling?

At 23 years old, I was in good health and had no trouble with the intense physical aspects of the course. Clive was older than me and not quite as fit, struggling with the long treks and scrambling over high walls. Even so, we both made it through the selection process and earned ourselves a spot in the training programme, setting us on the path to our respective futures.

The only downside of forming such a close bond with Rex was that I had to part ways with him when it was time for me to leave. It was the first but not the last time I would form a close bond with a dog.

Roy was a great teacher, and I will always be thankful for

the skills and tips he taught me. He judged me worthy as a dog handler and gave me the confidence to become the best handler I could be, however long that took. Thankfully, a dog handler in Huddersfield was due to retire soon, which meant I would have my first police dog in no time. I couldn't contain my enthusiasm!

CHAPTER SEVEN

FIRST DOG – STORM

In March 1978, I was notified that I would be attending a 13-week initial training course in July. I was then asked if I'd be willing to take a six-month-old German Shepherd puppy into my home and care for it until the course began, which didn't require much time for me to say, "Yes, please."

In a flash, a large wooden kennel with an attached run was erected in my back garden, and on 10th March, Storm arrived. He was one of the first puppies bred by our force, having been sired by a working police dog and mothered by the pet bitch of Geordie the kennel man. Of the seven puppies they had produced, only two were suitable for training, so his brother Zeus was assigned to an experienced handler and Storm to me.

When I took possession of Storm, I was eager to show him off to my wife. She was in the hospital at the time, preparing for the birth of our second baby. I recall her peering through the hospital window, seemingly as enthusiastic as me about our new family member, though perhaps not quite as much after being in the hospital for a week on bed rest. She looked completely drained.

Two days later, we welcomed another healthy baby into the world: a brother for our two-year-old daughter.

With our two kids, a new dog and our new lifestyle, the following months were undoubtedly hectic. I was still working as a beat officer, and Storm usually came to work with me, where I was able to leave him in one of the station's police dog kennels until I got time to walk him.

Although it proved difficult at times, caring for Storm was enjoyable, and I built an increasingly strong relationship with him over the next few months.

July arrived quickly and I began my basic training with Storm. By the end of the 13-week course, Storm and I would hopefully become a certified team.

Our instructor was Vinny, a slightly built man with a swarthy complexion and a thick South Yorkshire accent, perfect for barking instructions. There were three other handlers on the course: Big Bob, Dave and Denver, all experienced handlers. Storm's brother Zeus was also on the course, being handled by Denver.

The three veterans initially made me feel a bit awkward, not only because of their vast experience but also because of the stories they told about working with previous dogs. But I soon realised that some of Big Bob's tall tales were largely bullshit and the phrase, "Nowt here for me, kid" kept springing to mind.

We started the training with basic commands such as walking to heel, sitting, staying, lying down and standing. We also trained in agility techniques such as hurdling over three-foot obstacles, scaling six-foot walls and jumping across a distance of nine feet.

Other exercises included searching for both people and property in various environments such as buildings, open fields and wooded areas.

A special harness was used for the tracking exercise which involved following a scent across grassy terrain. Attempting to buckle the harness and keep an excited hound in line during this experience was an act of absolute artistry and something I initially failed at miserably!

The idea is that the dog will track not only the human scent as it has been transferred to the earth, but also crushed grass and insects below where the foot stands on the ground. It's much harder for a dog to pursue scent on a hard surface, and this skill is developed at a more advanced phase of the dog's training.

The goal of training the dog for criminal work was to develop its skills in chasing and detaining criminals by biting on the right arm. The process began through play by using a dummy arm as a toy for the dog to bite, transitioning onto a leather sleeve worn on the right arm. This was then gradually intensified until the dog was able to successfully apprehend armed criminals by chasing them down and biting them.

For the first couple of weeks, I had a tough time with all the exercises and I found it hard to keep up, not being a natural dog handler. Most of the other dogs seemed to be progressing just fine, but Storm was an exception. Part of this may have been my lack of knowing how to communicate properly with him, but he never seemed to have the desired spirit for play or aggression, and no matter what the other students would do to try and coax some out of him, he wouldn't even bark. After two weeks or so, Vinny realised that Storm would never make the required grade, and so his role on the course was terminated; Storm not Vinny's. This saddened me since I'd come to form a bond with him; Storm, not Vinny.

Disregarding the circumstances that had occurred with Storm, I moved onward and upward. Denver was apparently in some sort of trouble and had been kicked out of the dog section. Though I didn't know the full story, it seemed to involve 'shagging' in some capacity. In any case, as a result of all this, his dog Zeus was re-assigned to me. This prospect seemed far better at first, since all the training exercises were more advanced and at least he would bark when required.

Dave ran into some physical problems with his dog and also had to leave the course, so it was just me and Big Bob trapped together. He went on and on about how amazing his previous dog was; apparently it had caught thousands of criminals, bit most of them too, and was one of the top dogs in civilian and police trials. I lost count of the times I heard his thick Yorkshire accent exclaim:

"That's a reyt dog tha' knows. [*That was a right dog, you know.*] He could jump through a doughnut tied to two bits of string!" Okay, that last detail was made up, but fuck me, there really wasn't anything that reyt dog couldn't do. I am pretty sure this top dog never even left the police van.

During the course, I discovered that many handlers prioritised dog trials much more than actually catching criminals, which didn't sit well with me.

Despite all the problems on the course, Big Bob and I graduated with our fully-fledged police dogs. Zeus had been trained in all the skills we needed, and his obedience and tracking were especially impressive. What could possibly go wrong? Well, as it turned out, plenty …

CHAPTER EIGHT

POLICE DOG ZEUS

After graduating from the course, I returned to Huddersfield with my fully trained dog, excited as to what lay ahead. Dave, an experienced handler, mentored me for a few weeks. His dog was Zeus's dad, but you could never tell by looking at them.

The division was divided into four sub-divisions, and there were ten handlers in total. Dave didn't have any time for most of the other handlers, branding them as the 'too hot/too cold' or 'too wet/too dry' or 'nowt here for me, kid' kind of handlers.

One of the older handlers was like the Olympic flame; he never went out. Every time I saw him, he was in the office, reading a newspaper and smoking. He wouldn't look out of the window in the morning, otherwise he would have had nothing to do in the afternoon.

I soon realised that Dave was right, and I wanted to be like him: a practical dog handler who actually worked to catch criminals, not just to scoop prizes at dog trials. I reckoned I could do both, which proved to be another misconception on my part. Although training seemed to be progressing, a few things started to concern me during certain real-life incidents.

The first was when we went with CID to arrest a particularly well-known violent criminal. Two detectives went to the door and, sure enough, when the man was arrested, he became aggressive. I approached with Zeus, who wouldn't bark despite my encouragement. I felt as if he would have run off had he not been on a lead. The villain kicked Zeus, who made no attempt to retaliate which was disconcerting to say the least. It was also embarrassing especially as one of the CID present was Derek, who was later to become my best friend.

Another time, we searched a large market hall after a burglary had occurred and somehow missed the burglar hiding inside. During the search, Zeus never gave any indication of detecting human scent even though at a later date, CID inquiries led to the arrest of the culprit, and while being interviewed he claimed that the dog had been very close to him at some point during our search.

After speaking with the training school about my concerns, I was told he was simply inexperienced and would learn as he matured. Despite my doubts, I accepted what the highly regarded dog trainers told me.

We also re-enacted similar training scenarios in order to see if he could perform them properly, which he did. I continued to work with him up until 1981, but he wasn't tested extensively during that time. Even so, we still had some success in tracking down suspects, and we helped make several arrests, but nothing of great note.

I did take part in a couple of dog trials, and although his obedience was okay, I didn't enjoy the experience and realised it wasn't for me.

CHAPTER NINE

WHERE DID IT ALL GO WRONG?

I worked with Zeus for almost two years, yet I never fully trusted him during potentially violent confrontations. His barks during crowd disturbances, such as at football matches, were more like a polite request to leave rather than a "Fuck off, you cretins" type of bark.

The training school dismissed my concerns by saying he was still maturing and he did always perform well during training. Quite often I wondered how old he would be before fully maturing.

It all came to a head early in 1981. One night shift, we attended a domestic disturbance where a man stood on the doorstep and was threatening officers with a knife in one hand and a golf club in the other.

When I arrived, I got the dog out of the van, wishing I could say, "Nowt here for me, kid," and fuck off. However, it was my job, so I went forward, being as aggressive as I could and shouting at him to put the weapons down.

He was incoherently shouting something, and the only words I could decipher were f*** and c***. I attempted to chase him back into the house, but Zeus had different plans.

He kept pulling me on the lead, nearly tripping me up, as he wanted to run away no matter how hard I tried to get him back in the house. I felt threatened by the whole situation, but luckily, the other officers managed to restrain him. Several other officers witnessed this, including my former inspector, who had warned me long ago against wasting my career. At that moment, I felt embarrassed and wondered if he may have been right.

My embarrassment soon turned to anger as my supposedly well-trained dog put not only me but my colleagues in a life-threatening situation.

Later that same night, I caught a burglar descending from a roof via a drainpipe. Maybe there was a chance I could restore a bit of pride? Following my orders, he climbed down, but just as before, Zeus showed no inclination to attack him. As soon as his feet touched the ground, he brushed past Zeus, sprinting off down the road.

I commanded Zeus to "Stop him!" as per training, but he just ran alongside him, making no attempt to detain him. The burglar darted down an alley and by the time I arrived, he had vanished without a trace. Zeus stood by the wall, looking completely dumbfounded. Once more, my initial emotion was embarrassment, after which only anger remained.

Before going off duty, I was summoned to see the inspector.

Even though he didn't come out and say it, I could tell by his face that he believed I was wasting my career as he told me he would be submitting a report to the higher-ups in the dog section about both incidents, so I kept my emotions in check by saying nothing. In the long run, he did me a massive favour, although I didn't realise it at the time.

Driving home, I felt humiliated and was seething with anger. I was emotionally exhausted and unable to sleep. My wife tried to console me, but I was too deep in my own thoughts to listen. Even though I kept convincing myself that there was nothing more I could have done, I still felt despondent about the future.

It was barely noon when the dog section inspector, Ian, called me. He was a pleasant, down-to-earth chap, cutting straight to the point. He asked what had happened with Zeus, and I explained everything that had occurred in detail. He decided to take Zeus off duty immediately and arranged for me to attend the dog training school on the following Monday.

He was incredibly understanding and didn't make me feel any more shitty than I already did.

The same day, another handler arrived to take Zeus away, and I felt as if I had let him down. I didn't question where he was going or what would happen to him and at that moment I didn't really care, which I now feel terrible about. Afterwards I came to the conclusion that it was the training school that had let both of us down. I now know that Zeus would never have made an effective police dog and should never have been selected for training.

The remainder of the weekend was spent evaluating my

options. Should I stay as a dog handler, go back to patrol work, try something new, or even quit? I was feeling down and didn't have enough experience to understand why this had happened.

Through more understanding, I have observed that dogs possess the same instinctive fight-or-flight reaction as humans. Zeus's initial response was always to take flight, and no amount of training could alter his natural survival instinct. You can simulate many different scenarios in training sessions, but you cannot replicate the emotions of a real-life violent encounter with adrenaline and fear involved, which have a powerful effect on both humans and dogs. A perfect police dog must possess the will to fight first and foremost, as and when required.

When Monday morning came around, I went to the dog training school, unsure of what I wanted my fate to be. I thought that perhaps I did want to stay as a handler, but I never again wanted to experience the same emotions as that night.

I stepped into the canteen to find a strange atmosphere lingering in the air. Was it my imagination, or did everybody turn silent on my arrival? My insecurities and embarrassment got the better of me as I wondered what they were all thinking. Perhaps some of them knew what it was like to be in my shoes.

My initial course instructor, Vinny, came in, proclaiming in his thick South Yorkshire accent, "I allas knew that dog would let thi darn." [*I always knew that dog would let you down.*]

Perhaps he said this in front of others to prevent me from reacting by punching him on the fucking nose. If he thought that, why was I ever allowed out with a well-trained but practically inadequate dog that might potentially put me and others in danger?

If only Denver hadn't been caught shagging, I wouldn't have been in that predicament.

CHAPTER TEN

BLUE

After a pot of tea and more red-faced conversations in the canteen, I attended a meeting with Inspector Ian and Big Bob, who had taken up the role of instructor after Roy's retirement. My friend Clive from the suitability course had also been caught with his pants around his ankles, and he too was leaving the section meaning that his dog, Blue, was in the kennels, waiting for the right man to adopt him. The offer was made for me to take him and join a two-week refresher course with Big Bob as the instructor the following week.

I'd had the privilege of doing some training with Clive and Blue, so I knew he was a great dog. His level of obedience and tracking were, I would say, average, but his searching and criminal work skills were top-notch. He also had a fearsome reputation for biting perpetrators of violence. During a training exercise acting as a criminal, Blue's bite felt like being chewed by a crocodile, which gave me the confidence I needed to remain a dog handler.

Apart from once again having to listen to the endless stories from Big Bob about his previous dogs, the prospects appeared positive.

I accepted the offer and went to meet Blue in the kennel, entering as I had been instructed on my suitability course. This time around, it was much easier, and I immediately felt a connection with him. We took a walk down Shit Alley, and I had to shovel his poo into one of the strategically placed buckets; someone else would have to empty it later, I thought, while retching.

I spent about an hour playing with him, throwing a ball, getting him to chase me, and generally having fun. I drove home afterwards in anticipation of introducing him to my family. Any worries I had were quickly put to rest; he was accepted by the wife and kids right away, and he seemed quite content to be a part of our home. We all grew comfortable together very quickly.

The first week I spent with him was dedicated to getting acquainted and creating a bond through play, brushing, exercising and feeding him. His diet was a hefty one and a half pounds of raw meat and biscuits once daily. The first time I fed him was a real jaw-dropping moment as he devoured everything in around 30 seconds. It was like watching a vacuum cleaner inhaling trash, and it was so entertaining that it became a spectacle for visitors to our house.

At the time, I couldn't explain why, but he had an unmistakable air of confidence. His face was a golden colour, and his body was mostly golden with a patch of black on his back. He had a great chunk missing from one of his ears from a previous dog fight, and although he wasn't the prettiest, he certainly exuded a certain aura from his muscular frame. This gave me a sense of assurance, knowing our relationship would mean no more work incidents that would leave me with negative emotions.

The following week, I joined two more handlers and Big Bob for a two-week refresher course. As ever, Big Bob entertained us with stories of his three canine partners, two of whom had already retired. The third, a dedicated Labrador drug-search dog, was already responsible for taking down Pablo Escobar's Yorkshire branch by finding his cartel's drug stash. Big Bob was a master when it came to handling dogs, and he let everyone know it.

Right away, it was clear that Blue was quite different from Zeus. His obedience and tracking skills weren't up to the same level, but he excelled at searching and criminal work. It seemed like he was actually enjoying what he was doing, unlike a robot simply programmed to do its task.

He was a natural, and I couldn't wait to try him out for real. In training, when shouting out a challenge for the criminals to stop running or come out of hiding, he was straining on the end of the lead, waiting to be released while barking aggressively. All the power had to go somewhere, and it usually ended with him flattening the person running or trying to get into their hiding place at full force. Okay, he was difficult to control, but I was prepared for that.

Having completed a pleasurable two-week course, I returned to Division to start work with Blue, and I was confident we could deal with the challenges ahead.

Over the few years we were together, we faced many challenging incidents, but we handled them all confidently. It was during this time that I really began to learn about police dog handling and adapted my training methods more to the practical side of job. I knew it was important for Blue to be obedient, but I never resorted to forceful tactics such as using a choke chain to make him walk closely to heel. If I had, he probably would have challenged me and made things more difficult. Instead, we maintained a positive working relationship and became a formidable duo.

We were responsible for helping keep the peace in a number of situations, including football matches and the chaos that often unfolded on Friday and Saturday nights. We searched buildings, woodlands and other open areas, resulting in many arrests. Those who tried to resist or became violent usually found themselves at the local hospital, getting stitches and a tetanus injection.

Violence was rife in the 1980s, particularly at football matches. Huddersfield Town versus Leeds United was a prime example of this. The tension and atmosphere between fans before, during and after the game were obvious. One day, I happened to be on escort duty after the game, ensuring a large group of Leeds supporters made it safely to the railway station. Suddenly, some of them became violent and tried to break free from our cordon, rushing back towards the Huddersfield idiots. It was then that Blue bit one of these troublemakers in the stomach, causing him to immediately drop to the ground. After I managed to prise

Blue off him, some of his friends intervened, dragging him away and disappearing quickly into the rampaging mob before we could arrest him. I spotted an enormous crescent-shaped bite mark on his abdomen before he was hauled out of sight, and despite making enquiries to find and arrest him, I never saw him again.

I recall one moment very distinctly: around three o'clock one morning, I was sent out to search a park for a missing, vulnerable 14-year-old girl. The only tools at my disposal were my dog and a torch, so I set off into the night, guiding Blue with calls and whistles that echoed through the silence. He stopped, lifted his head and twitched his ears before taking off and entering the toilet block. Inside, he gave a low-pitched bark, at which point I joined him, and there was the young girl, curled up on the ground. He stopped barking and, having done his job, lay down, totally relaxed. Thankfully, we had found her safe, saving her family from distress and her from any harm.

To me, this shows how a police dog with a good temperament can distinguish between violent and non-threatening people.

A knocked over dustbin completely distracted my four-legged partner during another search. John, one of my good friends, accompanied me on the case. I shone my torch and saw Blue had picked up a large chop bone; apart from chasing criminals, food was his first love. *Bollocks,* I thought, *I've got to get that off him before it gets inhaled by the Dyson vacuum cleaner.* I managed to put a lead on him, tightened it, and said,

"Leave." He gave me a very bemused look, as if to say, "Not a fucking chance." As he chomped down on the bone, my shouts grew louder, as did his growls. I asked John to hold the lead, but he also replied, with equal vigour, "Not a fucking chance!"

With all my strength pushing him against a wall – Blue, not John – I yanked the bone away after much pulling and tugging. His eyes were glazing over rapidly, and he kept trying to break free from my grip; I had to keep hold of his head so he couldn't move!

Eventually his growling stopped, his eyes cleared, and when he calmed, I let him go, and everything was once again okay. My so-called mate said, "I thought you were going to kill him." My reply was, "I thought I was going to have to." I think Blue was already planning his revenge.

Another memorable incident was in the early hours when I got a report of a woman screaming. Not knowing what was happening, I arrived to find a sergeant and PC already on the scene and was immediately sent to the bottom of a short street, to stay there and not allow anybody in or out. The sergeant and the PC went to the top of the street with the same brief. I had to observe one of the back-to-back houses where it appeared there had been a shooting. More intelligence was coming over the radio, and we were informed that the screaming woman's ex-boyfriend had broken into her house, confronted her and her new boyfriend in bed, shooting him in the head. It later transpired that he had then taken her into the bathroom and raped her, after which he told her to go and ring the police. This was in the 1980s, prior to mobile phones, so she ran to the nearest phone box and dialled 999. The operator could make no sense of her screaming, and that is why we were only sent to a report of a screaming woman, not knowing the full story.

Everything seemed quiet and still as police officers cordoned off the area. I remained in cover, with Blue by my side, my thoughts racing ahead of me, imagining the worst-case scenario. We were unsure if the shooter was still in the house or had escaped somehow; but what if he ran out of the house, all guns blazing? This thought and others kept me on my toes. More intelligence was coming through the radio and it became known who the suspected shooter was. His car was found approximately 100 yards away, indicating he hadn't driven away and could still be inside the house, so everyone remained in cover keeping vigilant.

When the firearms team arrived, they formulated a plan to search the house, and to increase their chances of success, they asked me if I was willing to let my dog search the house while I stayed outside, protected by an armed officer. The house was a small one-story dwelling with a bedroom and bathroom upstairs and an open kitchen and lounge downstairs. The firearms sergeant's curiosity led him to ask what my dog would do if he stumbled upon a dead body. My curiosity was also piqued; after all, Blue had not been trained for such a task.

Would he bark if he found someone dead? Would he try to detain them by biting them if they were alive, or would he try eating them? If this had been his choice, it wouldn't have taken long.

These posed unsettling questions since it meant putting him in potential harm's way, but then again, that is the life of a police dog.

My minder and I crept along the wall, stopping at the partially opened door. As I called out a challenge for anyone inside to surrender themselves, my pulse started racing, causing the dog's excitement to intensify as I released him. The hairy-arsed copper grabbed my collar and yanked me back as I instinctively went to follow Blue.

Keeping myself concealed, I was able to spy through a small crack between the door and the frame. It was a bit disconcerting but out of the corner of my eye I could see a firearm pointing into the house from just behind my left shoulder, and others aiming towards the windows. I saw Blue run around the downstairs room and kitchen before climbing the stairs. All I could hear were his feet pounding against the flooring, followed by complete silence. I was encouraging him, but he stayed quiet, so after a few minutes I called him back to me, to see his golden face smeared with red, shiny blood.

I couldn't be sure if the gunman was still inside, alive, but I would have expected a reaction from Blue had he been, and I expressed my thoughts to the firearms sergeant. However, it was evident that something terrible had transpired, and with the mood remaining tense, the firearms team conducted a thorough tactical search where they encountered the new boyfriend dead in bed and the ex-boyfriend, who had succumbed to a self-inflicted gunshot wound, in the bathroom.

We breathed a collective sigh of relief when we realised no one else was involved in the situation, meaning we were all safe.

Before attending a debriefing, I took Blue for a well-earned shit, also taking the time to clean the blood from his face, wondering whether he had started snacking on one of the bodies.

Back at the station, I had my own stress relieving clear out before attending the debriefing. The firearms sergeant thanked me for my role in the incident but mentioned they couldn't find the boyfriend's eyes. I replied with more dark humour that I would check Blue's turds over the next few days to see if they showed up. I had visions of lifting his tail while grooming him to see an eye peering at me from out of his arsehole.

This and similar incidents led to more training for dogs and firearms team members, resulting in dedicated firearms dogs as well as improved search tactics.

In spite of Blue's intimidating size and sometimes aggressive duties as a police dog, he was a well-behaved, gentle giant. I would often present talks at schools and to visitors at the police station (the non-handcuffed kind of people). During these presentations, Blue would either sit or lie down quietly while I shared facts about a police dog's capabilities. One time, I was speaking to a group of young teenagers and their teachers in the station yard. In the midst of the presentation, they started laughing loudly, and I could hear the sound of splashing water. I looked to my left and saw Blue squatting with what can only be described as the contents of the River Ganges cascading from his arse. The worst case of ~~diar, dior, dihaho~~ shits I'd ever seen or smelled, for that matter. I concluded the talk, made my apologies, and said my goodbyes with a "Don't slip in that on your way out." Yet another embarrassing moment in the life of a dog handler. I had to clean my boots, but with no Kiwi available, I just used a brush and a hosepipe, which I also used to swill down the yard.

CHAPTER ELEVEN

MINERS' STRIKE 1984-1985

During the miners' strike of 1984–85, my experience with Blue was particularly difficult. I remember working for hours on end, often twelve, fourteen, or sometimes even sixteen-hour shifts. I was always on call at a moment's notice and had little time for family life, and when I *did* have some, I was too exhausted to appreciate it.

Alan and his dog Duke were our partners for most of the strike, and fortunately we all got along well.

On night shifts, it was especially dull; our duties were guarding the pits, staying awake to deter any prospective saboteurs. On one occasion, our sergeant caught us snoring like pigs in our van, our home for almost 12 months; he was laughing like a rabid hyena at us from outside the van window. It was unusual that neither of the dogs barked as they usually did when anyone approached the van. The sounds and smells coming from our vehicle must have been horrendous, with two men and two dogs snoring and farting for mind-numbing hours on end.

We used to while away the boring hours by playing games, cracking jokes, and even singing. We wrote some of our own tunes and made up silly games about our strike experiences. They weren't always politically correct, but we got a good laugh out of them as we tried to boost our morale.

When there was some down-time during the day, we would pass the time playing cricket with an improvised bat using a piece of wood or a pick-axe handle. I recall having a full-blown football match at the beginning of the strike. There must have been 20 players on each team, all wearing police uniforms and big boots. As is typical for some police footballers, some were trying to kick the shit out of each other.

On certain occasions, the work became terrifying. One morning, just as it was breaking dawn, we were in a wood bordering a pit in South Yorkshire. It was eerily silent, apart from the sound of missiles rustling through the leaves as they rained down on us. Bricks, bottles, and, ironically, large lumps of coal were thrown, but fortunately, despite being hit a few times, none of us were injured, though that was more due to sheer luck than anything else. A few of my colleagues encountered an ambush on their way to a colliery also located in South Yorkshire. The police vehicles suffered extensive damage, and some of the lads suffered injuries after physically battling with striking miners.

We often faced angry pickets, using our dogs to keep them from obstructing the transportation of working miners through the pit gates, always a scary experience.

June 18, 1984, is a day that has been forever etched in my mind. I was present at the so-called "Battle of Orgreave", a

British Steel coking plant where coal was turned into coke to be used for steel production. When we arrived, it was supposed to be a quiet day, with just a few pickets attempting to block trucks from delivering coal to the plant.

We had no idea what was in store for us as around: 8,000 pickets showed up. Initially, it was noisy but peaceful until the trucks arrived and then all hell broke loose. The miners' leader, Arthur Scargill, was arrested, boosting police morale but agitating the pickets more. As a result, we spread out with our dogs across an open field to stop them from advancing any further. I was transfixed watching this dream-like scene unfold before my eyes, an experience I never wanted to go through again.

Although I'm not going to get into the politics of this conflict, it was an experience that most of my colleagues didn't want any part of, and I'm sure the miners didn't either. In the end, nobody involved came out looking good.

The only silver lining, personally, was the overtime that came from it. With the extra money, we were able to take a family holiday to Majorca, our first time flying.

I worked with Blue until 1986, when his age and declining energy levels put him over the retirement threshold for police dogs. His work was still excellent, but it wasn't enough to keep him on the force any longer. Unfortunately, I don't want to say much about what happened to Blue after he retired as it goes against my values; however, it was not a pleasant outcome.

CHAPTER TWELVE

ZAXON MOONRAKER

At the start of this story, I mentioned 1986 as the year I began a new relationship. Previously, I had worked with three dogs – two were terrible police dogs, but they would have made lovely cuddly pets. The third was the best, but I hadn't trained any of them from the start. Two of them I only got due to sexual shenanigans. Thus, this was an entirely fresh start in the section, despite having been a handler for eight years.

During the summer of '86, I encountered my new dog for the first time. A colleague, Jeffers, assessed his suitability to be trained as a police dog. The previous owners could no longer look after him as he had grown too big for the flat they were living in. He was a 12-month-old striking black and tan German Shepherd, and the force paid thirty pounds for him after he passed a rigorous assessment.

He had an air about him just like Blue did when I first encountered him. He gave off a strong, confident aura and looked the part – the only downside being his ridiculous kennel name, Zaxon Moonraker. I could never understand why owners give their dogs such ridiculous titles. Without hesitation, I decided to refer to him as Zac!

Some of the other instructors, including Big Bob and Vinny, whose nose I still had an urge to punch, were studying the Kennel Club pedigree certificate, spouting off about all the sires and dams they knew in the blood line. Fuck me, their vast knowledge of all the names on the pedigree certificate was endless, going right back to Baron Von Shithousen, a very great-great and even greater grandfather of Zaxon Moonraker. I tried to show enthusiasm for their conversation, but it really meant nothing to me and, I'm sure, to Zac. Nevertheless, they appeared pleased with themselves as they shared their considerable expertise.

It didn't take me long to learn about Zac's personality and introduce him to my family. They instantly became enamoured with him, and their admiration for him only grew over the years. As you read on, hopefully you will get a sense of why he was so important to me and why he plays a major role in my narrative.

After spending a few weeks getting to know Zac and including him in our family routines, we started a 13-week basic dog training course. I was excited as he would be the first dog I had trained from scratch; all he knew prior to that was how to sit or give us his paw. In the weeks leading up to the course, I worked on his recall by letting him off the lead, calling out his name or whistling to get his attention, and on doing so, immediately moving away in the opposite direction so that he would follow me. When he got to me, I praised him with a "good boy" and a stroke. It became a game that we both loved playing. By the time the training course started, Zac was following my directions every time. This was thanks to my suitability instructor, Roy, who taught me the importance of recall and how to teach it without formal training.

I engaged in playful exercises with Zac, enticing him to chase after toys that I threw. Occasionally, I would purposely throw a toy into the long grass, prompting him to utilise his incredible cold wet nose to locate it. * Moreover, I repeated a similar exercise with other objects such as wallets and keys, anything that held human scent. This allowed me to educate Zac on how to recover scent bearing items. As for testing his biting abilities, I fashioned a dummy sleeve and engaged in tug-of-war games with him. Furthermore, I would run away while holding the sleeve to my right side, enabling Zac to learn how to pursue and grasp it. While these weren't formal training sessions, they served as opportunities for Zac to enhance his natural senses in preparation for future challenges. Both Zac and I thoroughly enjoyed these activities, reinforcing the bond we were developing. Prior to commencing the training course, I also dedicated some time to basic obedience training, but the focus primarily remained on refining his natural senses.

> *Have you ever wondered why a dog's nose is wet and cold? The mucus coating on their noses helps them to smell better by collecting scent particles. German Shepherds, for example, have around 225 million scent receptors compared to humans who only have 6 million.*
>
> *Throughout my work with dogs, I was always impressed by the capabilities of their noses; they can be used to detect drugs, explosives, corpses, firearms, and even money! When I was an instructor, I*

initiated training for all West Yorkshire drugs dogs so that they could sniff out firearms. After my retirement, this program was taken even further so that they are now trained to detect cash, too. Dogs are being trained in all walks of life, even detecting diseases in humans such as cancerous cells.

Surely we have a lot more to explore in the field of a dog's olfactory sense?

CHAPTER THIRTEEN

INITIAL TRAINING (AGAIN)

September 1986

Jeffers was our instructor, and there were four students, myself included, that took part: Harry, Roger, and Steve all had previous experience working with police dogs.

The 13 weeks went well, as all of the dogs performed better than expected. We all became close and had some great laughs, with none of the typical blowhard stories I'd heard on other courses. Everyone seemed more relaxed on this course than any other I'd been on before, which was reflected in the quality and success of the training.

Each morning, Zac would go through the necessary formal obedience training, and while his results weren't quite as impressive as some of the other dogs, it was undeniable that he had a special flair for tracking and searching, along with performing criminal work with enthusiasm, panache and the necessary aggression. I may be a little biased, but his love of work, combined with his natural ability, made him one of the finest police dogs I'd ever met.

By the end of the course, Zac had become a master of chasing and detaining criminals. Despite not being the largest dog, his speed and impeccable timing would often result in the criminal being taken to the floor, something that continued throughout his service until he aged and lost some of his agility.

Harry, Steve and Roger commuted to the course from home, yet I was required to stay at Bishopgarth Police Training School located a few miles away from the dog school. This was due to the fact that three students from Malaysia were taking part in an eight-week drugs dog search course and were also staying there. The powers that be needed someone dependable to take the three students under their wing, teach them about the culture and history of our country, and also look after and care for them.

Bollocks to that! We were out for some laughs and lots of fun, and if they'd wanted somebody dependable, perhaps they should have looked for someone else.

We were also expected to return to the dog school in the evening for one last walk with our four-legged friends, for which I was issued a Ford Transit dog van to chauffeur them around.

Jai, Tchew and Zie – their names, not pronouns – were all officers of the Malaysian customs service, and it soon became clear to me that there was tension between them. I suspected it had something to do with Jai's Indian background since Tchew and Zie seemed to show disrespect towards him.

Despite this, they had a great sense of humour, and I grew close to Jai. He even stayed with my family for a weekend, during which he cooked us a delicious Malaysian meal, one we still fondly remember.

Once, we took him to the east coast and explored Flamborough Head together. His breath was taken away by the chilly air that swept across his face. We stood atop the majestic cliffs together, and I thought he was going to pass out with the polar temperature and hurricane-force wind. For us, it was just a normal autumnal two-layer day with a stiff breeze.

He was such a wonderful person, one of the few that left you feeling better after meeting them. He invited us to his wedding in Malaysia, but unfortunately the miners hadn't been on strike again, so we were unable to afford it. He did, however, send us a picture of him and his gorgeous wife on their special day.

Each morning, every handler was responsible for cleaning out their own dog's kennel. Tchew's Golden Labrador had the habit of messing in his kennel every night, so one evening someone placed a massive papier-mâché turd in it. The next morning, Tchew saw the enormous faux excrement and ran out of the kennel, shouting in his Malaysian accent, "Ohhhh, big shit, fucking big shit!" There was also a gut-wrenching stench added to the scene as the dog had done not quite as big a shit in the far side of the kennel.

We all pissed ourselves laughing at his reaction, especially when Big Bob entered the kennel and returned carrying the artificial bowel movement in his hand. Tchew was retching to the point of almost spewing before he realised it wasn't real shit, taking it in good humour and laughing as he cleared the smaller shit away.

When their course concluded after two months, they returned home to Malaysia with their dogs in tow. They were hopeful of being able to catch some dastardly drug smugglers, who could face the death penalty if found guilty of transporting narcotics in their country.

Let's resume to my basic course: everything was going well in all departments except for control after Zac had made a bite, whether it was on someone running away or someone facing us with a weapon. In such cases, police dogs have to let go once they hear the command "Leave!" This wasn't easy with Zac because he adored biting and didn't want to release his grip. He'd already caught the target, so why should he give it up? All the brains in the training school couldn't come up with an answer. We tried pulling him, prodding him, and shouting louder, until the esteemed Big Bob had the brilliant idea of hitting him across the flanks with a stick.

He had used this old-fashioned police dog training method on his previous dogs, but it took a large piece of 3 x 2 wood, not a measly stick. "Hardest dogs in't force tha' knows," he boomed in his broad accent.

But did it work on Zac? No, did it bollocks. It just made him hang on harder in an attempt to kill the thing he believed was causing him pain.

I'd never understood why food rewards were not common practice when it came to training police dogs, a method I thought could have worked with Zac.

In the end, I had to resort to bribery to get him to release his grip on the criminal's arm. He was obsessed with his favourite toy, a big blue rubber bone he used for tracking, fetching and tug-of-war games. So, when I commanded "Leave", I waved the bone in front of him so he could see it. Once he released the sleeve, I threw the bone and watched as he happily chased it, his mind now focused on something else. This strategy always worked great when practising our criminal work exercises, so in this case, bribery was more effective than brute force.

With no sexual shenanigans and all the dogs remaining fit, all four of us and our dogs managed to complete the gruelling but satisfying 13-week training course. I was pleased with how things had gone and felt confident that Zaxon Moonraker could handle whatever work came our way. Getting control over him wasn't my top priority, but it was high on the agenda.

Now we had to concentrate on making the transition from training to real-life events with emotions, adrenaline and violence, and I must admit there was still some trepidation although I was more confident this time around, having more experience and a far superior partner. As it turned out, I didn't have to worry at all.

CHAPTER FOURTEEN

SERGEANT NEV AND

THE POLICE DOG DISPLAY TEAM

After a successful basic course, I returned to Division confident and looking forward to any challenges that lay ahead.

At the same time, our divisional dog sergeant, Nev, began to provide me with advice and guidance for the progression of our training. He was slightly built and softly spoken; he was also an exceptional handler and the best sergeant I ever worked under. Nothing could rattle him, and his mere presence improved the lives of those around him.

He was one of the earliest body detection dog handlers enlisted in our force, and in December 1988, he was sent to Lockerbie, Scotland, to locate victims of the Pan Am Flight 103 terrorist bombing. His search dog was a border collie named Jan. For his incredible services at the time, he received the British Empire Medal.

In 1979, I was with Nev during a search to locate a four-year-old girl who had gone missing the previous night on a stroll with her dog. While we were searching through a fleet of Portakabins located near the Huddersfield Town football stadium, Nev summoned me over. My eyes widened as I gazed into one of the cabins, observing a deceased little girl inside with a dog. She was naked, her body covered in scratches, some of her hair pulled out – all signs that pointed to foul play. That scene has cemented itself in my mind and will never be forgotten, no matter how hard I try.

We waited at the cabin until the major event team began to arrive. It later became clear that the girl had not been murdered; she had become accidentally locked in the cabin and, due to the cold of the night, had taken off her clothing – a symptom of exposure. It appeared that the dog had been trying to wake her up from her state of unconsciousness, sadly to no avail.

At the debriefing, there was an eerie silence; everybody was subdued without any of the customary dark humour. Everyone, myself included, sobbed and sniffled in the silence that draped over us. Even the toughest among us couldn't hold back their tears.

When I returned home after a long day, my daughter had just finished her first day at school. She was still in her crisp new uniform, full of enthusiasm from the day's events, but I couldn't bring myself to feel the same joy and struggled to respond to her excitement, something I regret to this day.

A range of emotions bubbled up within me, including sadness and anger, as I pondered the picture of a four-year-old child out for a stroll with her dog without her parents. It was undoubtedly the most heart-breaking moment I ever experienced in my job, worse even than when I attempted to save a woman who had been viciously stabbed and bludgeoned to death, her blood sprayed not only over the kitchen floor but the walls and ceiling, too. Her assailant was sitting calm and collected on the couch, waiting to be arrested which he duly was, without a fuss.

Nev was a great asset to Zac and me in terms of aiding our training programme. He also persuaded me to join the Police Dog Display Team. I'd expressed my reluctance before to involve myself in dog trials, but I was now willing to showcase our abilities to the public. During this period, the police had a good reputation with the community, which led us to do presentations at schools, galas, and an annual Police Day featuring police cars, horse displays and the most popular, dog demonstrations of obedience, agility and criminal work displays.

Throughout the displays, I embraced diverse roles, effortlessly transitioning from a cunning criminal to a skilled dog handler. But perhaps the most remarkable transformation was when I took on the persona of an ice cream seller. Dressed in an immaculate white coat, I proudly wheeled my ramshackle ice cream cart into the arena, energetically enticing customers with my frozen delights. Just as Inspector Ian's voice resounded over the Tannoy, instructing me to get out of the field, an unexpected commotion erupted. A woman's terrified shriek pierced the air as a brazen criminal snatched her handbag and swiftly darted across the arena.

I dropped the front door of the cart by quickly releasing a catch, and out jumped Zac like an Exocet missile, in hot pursuit of the dastardly villain. The audience erupted into cheers as Zac sank his teeth into his arm, dragging him to the ground.

After Zac had released him, thanks to the blue bone tucked up my sleeve, we strode off the arena to rapturous applause, feeling like a million pounds.

Hamish, a bloodhound, was acquired by the section to be used for tracking criminals over long distances or searching for missing people. His handler, Instructor Vinny, thought it would be a good idea to take Hamish to exhibitions. He did a grand impersonation of Sherlock Holmes, fully kitted out with the classic deerstalker hat, cape and pipe, looking a complete twat as they ambled around the arena waving to the astonished crowd, Hamish slobbering his secretions everywhere. Hamish was never used for anything but training and, at the end of the day, it was simply a waste of taxpayers' money.

We designed an adventurous obstacle course filled with various challenges for our dogs: leaping over hurdles, jumping through hoops and running through a tunnel made from hessian fabric. The tunnel had an opening at the entrance and was closed off at the end, creating a thrilling experience as the dog ran through it. The hessian fabric would lift, revealing the dog's outline as it raced through.

During one of our training sessions, Zac encountered a

slight mishap. He somehow got stuck in the middle of the tunnel, causing him to panic and resort to pulling at the fabric. Thankfully, I was able to intervene just in time to prevent him from completely destroying it. I then assisted him in safely making his way out of the tunnel. Throughout the rest of the day, with the help of my initial training course buddy, Steve, we overcame the problem by bribing Zac through the tunnel with his treasured blue bone. It worked perfectly until he was going through it with ease. During the dress rehearsal, we completed the course in the fastest time, becoming favourites for the highly competitive race on the day.

On the day of a police display, everyone was engaging in the usual police banter, making inappropriate jokes and generally taking the piss out of each other.

Smart Terry was usually the centre of attention, as he was one of the most prolific piss-takers. Not so good when it was directed at him, though. He was always spotless, as if he'd never been involved in anything, always combing his shiny ebony hair, gleaming from the Grecian 2000 dye he obviously used. The obstacle course time trial was becoming more competitive as he had been the favourite to win until Zac's majestic performance the day before.

It was time to run, and Smart Terry was watching in anticipation, having already clocked an impressive time without dripping sweaty black hair dye down his well-chiselled face. Zac took off at an impressive speed, clearing all of the obstacles with ease. However, everything came to a grinding halt when he once again got stuck in the hessian tunnel, began to panic, and started ripping it apart. The race was a disaster, but we persevered and finished it in one piece, unlike the hessian tunnel. The audience guffawed loudly at our misfortunes but gave us a good round of applause for our efforts. As I left the arena, I noticed that Smart Terry was smirking as he won the competition again, which made me feel like 50 pence.

Smart Terry had a cunning plan to play a trick on me at the Leeds Police Day event. There were many big chiefs and other dignitaries there, so it was important that everything went perfectly. The hessian tunnel was showing signs of wear and tear and for some reason, I wasn't allowed to take part in the obstacle course on this occasion.

I was ready to use Zac to pursue a suspect across the arena and needed my blue bone as a bribe to get him to release the criminal. I frantically searched but couldn't find it, so I had to go ahead without it. Smart Terry had an evil sneer on his face as I entered the arena, and I finally realised where the bone had gone. I kept my composure and managed to give him a smile, but inside I was fuming. "You twat!"

Nevertheless, as they say in Hollywood, the show must go on, so I let Zac chase after the villain, which he did with his usual aplomb until he was brought to the ground. When I reached him, I clipped on his lead, commanding him to "leave." "No fucking way," was his silent reply, so I bent down and whispered in his ear. Immediately, he released, and we walked off to another round of cheers from the audience.

In the audience was my wife who asked what I had whispered to Zac in order to make him release his grip. The truth was, I hadn't said anything; I had just bitten the tip of his ear. Surprisingly, it worked on this occasion, but I promised myself it would never happen again.

The bone reappeared mysteriously in the back of my van, but Smart Terry never admitted to taking it, though we were all sure it was him. If only I could have found his Grecian 2000 hair dye!

One particular display team story that stands out in my mind was after a long day of training for a show, I wanted to scream at one particular handler. He droned on and on in his annoyingly loud southern drawl, volunteering to do all the exercises with his dog and act criminal for all the events, grating on my very last nerve.

All I could hear was, "I'll do this, I'll do that, I'll stick a brush up my arse and sweep the arena at the same time." Fuck me, give it a rest, and leave something for others to do.

I went home after a tiresome day and had a couple of beers, which inspired me to think of a brilliant idea.

"That southerner won't be able to do this!" I thought whilst chuckling to myself like a mischievous child. I took an egg and went into the front garden with Zac. My plan was to train him to retrieve it, at which point I would crack it, allowing him to eat the contents. With the wife and kids watching through the window, I soon had him gently holding the egg in his mouth without breaking it while I smiled towards the appreciative audience.

I progressed, commanding him to stay while I put the egg on the ground a few yards away. I sent him to retrieve it, and he quickly scooped it up, dropped it on the ground, greedily lapping up the contents.

I couldn't think of any more stupid tricks, so I thought, *Fuck it, I'll let him stick the brush up his arse!*

I went back in the house to "cracking that, Dad" and other egg-related yokes.

Overall, being part of the group was morale-boosting for everyone in the team, always joking around and engaging in spirited albeit sometimes good old inappropriate police banter!

CHAPTER FIFTEEN

INSPECTOR MICK

Early on in his career, Zac and I dealt with numerous incidents efficiently. We arrested many criminals for a variety of offences, searched buildings to find burglars, tracked suspects from scenes of crimes, and found stolen property. As I earlier stated, dogs never cease to amaze me with their fantastic sense of smell. One time, during a search after a burglary, Zac sniffed out something in the grass, and as I shone my torch towards it, I spotted an earring. How could he have smelled a scent on that? It was later identified by its owner as one of the stolen items. Unfortunately, we only found one, so perhaps she could wear it as a nose piercing or on some other part of her anatomy.

Despite his successful record, Zac had never really been put to the test in a truly violent situation since most people surrendered without a fight. We did have a few minor scuffles resulting in him nipping offenders, but none that posed any real threat to us. He was an intimidating presence when on patrol, dealing with crowds at football matches as well as rowdy individuals on Friday and Saturday nights; everyone seemed to behave themselves once they heard us barking out commands with Zac baring his 42 razor-sharp teeth.

It all changed in early 1988 when he had his first real experience of an extremely violent situation. We were supposed to be performing a display at a nearby school gala, so we prepared by having dinner in the police canteen: homemade pie, chips, peas and lashings of gravy, typical food for a police canteen. This fare was nicknamed 'football pie' due to the fact it was the only item on the menu prior to working a match, with a veggie option of chips and peas. Little did we know that these canteens would later be discontinued by the idiotic powers that be.

There were eight of us performing at the display, including a dog sergeant, a rather rotund, unfit man, although I'm trying to be kind in describing him here.

We were all feeling at ease with the prospect of an enjoyable afternoon when we received news that we should immediately make our way to Bradford for a reported riot. We discovered that it was caused by around 1000 Muslims who had set fire to a divisive book called *The Satanic Verses*, by the writer Salman Rushdie. Our sergeant didn't take too kindly to having our tasty lunch interrupted halfway through.

We arrived in a massive convoy of eight dog vans, all with flashing blue lights and blaring two-tones, which must have been an impressive sight. Upon arrival, we were greeted by an aggressive mob of young Asian men who were hurling objects at the police officers. I saw stones, beer bottles, and even a few pool balls thrown their way. The scene was chaotic; no one offered us instructions, so we made our own plan: use the dogs to form a line to push back the enraged crowd. We had to be careful, though; if anyone fell while advancing, they would be left vulnerable so it was executed by us moving slowly towards the rioters.

I saw around six men lift a bench up above their heads, and, as I was pretty sure it wasn't so they could move the seat to get a ringside view, I instinctively started to move towards them, the hair standing up on the back of my neck. As I did so, Zac leapt to his left at someone sprinting past me from behind, sinking his teeth into his stomach.

"Fuck me!" I cried out, only to cry an even louder "FUCK ME!" when I saw two silver pips on the shoulder of his police tunic. Zac had gone and taken a chomp out of an inspector; where the fucking hell did he come from?

The frenzied cries of the rioters quickly turned to laughter as they watched a panicked police dog handler attempting to pry his dog off a police inspector. His hold was like a fully tightened vice, and I had to use all my strength to free him. When he finally let go, the inspector stepped away with his tunic in shreds. It did cause the bench throwers to put their weapon down, probably to have a seat while they pissed themselves laughing at the chaotic scene. We proceeded cautiously with crowd control, and no one dared approach us after that, the rioters moving back in silence away from the dogs.

Once the commotion settled, I reported the inspector fiasco to our sergeant, who was now sweating profusely and quite probably starving. PC Smart Terry was there, looking like he had been stuck in his van for the duration, obsessively combing his beautiful dark locks. The sergeant asked me if we could forget it, and at that very moment, with adrenaline still flowing in my bloodstream, I felt a strong inclination to give him a smack in the kisser.

My four-legged partner-in-crime has just exhibited aggressive behaviour to an inspector! was my polite thought. However, what came out of my mouth was not so polite.

After a short time, another handler came to me and said, "I think I just found your inspector," pointing to a figure wearing a bright white and red shirt. As I thought he might blame Zac for the episode, I gestured for the sergeant to follow me for support as I approached the inspector. Before I got the chance to speak, he got the first word in.

"I apologise; I was so focused on catching those fuckers with the bench that I didn't even notice the dogs."

Surprised by his immediate admission, I quickly engaged in a pleasant encounter with him, advising him to get his wounds checked at a hospital and make sure his tetanus was up to date. His thick blue uniform likely shielded him from more severe injuries.

We exchanged names for our reports; his was Inspector Mick, a supervisor in the task force. Fortunately, this wasn't the only time I encountered Inspector Mick. I was impressed by him as both a leader and a person who accepted responsibility for their own actions. Not like some of the namby-pamby wankers I have come across who would drop you in it to save their own skin.

I returned home exhausted, though not pleased that my new friend had been injured. Zac, however, had received his first experience of biting human flesh in a high-octane situation and had reacted aggressively to it, which I found reassuring. He'd made the transition from training bites on a leather sleeve and nips to a full-blooded nibble, albeit on an innocent police inspector.

Years later, I had the opportunity to work at a Michael Jackson concert in Leeds, attached to a task force team. In charge of that team was none other than Inspector Mick. The moment he saw me, he said, "Keep that fucking dog away from me! I don't want Zacking again!" Everyone around us laughed, immersing us in a warm and friendly atmosphere. What a great guy, one who was obviously well-respected by his troops.

The rest of the concert was spent listening to Michael belting out *Billie Jean* and all his other classics – thrilling stuff!

Years later, I was dispatched to a firearms incident and assigned an armed nanny. After being briefed, we got into my van, him with his Heckler and Koch MP5 and me with my dog in tow. He then asked if he could take a picture of the dog at the end of the incident, which I found a weird request, but consented to anyway.

When I enquired why, he told me they were putting together a *This Is Your Life* book for their inspector, who was leaving the firearms unit to take another role. Evidently, this individual had been held in high regard within the task force and firearms unit, and the book was meant to commemorate his achievements while serving there.

"He was bitten by a police dog when attempting to contain a riot in Bradford," he then informed me.

"Inspector Mick?"

"Yes, do you know him?"

"Not only do I know him, it was my fucking dog that bit him!" I replied with glee.

He was ecstatic and couldn't wait to share the news with his co-workers when we got back to the station.

"We've got Zac!" he exclaimed with a massive grin. Everyone was euphoric and somebody took photos of Zac barking aggressively (with an actual camera; smartphones weren't a thing yet). They even asked me and Zac to join in on the leaving party, but I had commitments on the day. I imagined Eamon Andrews asking Inspector Mick if he could recall this voice: "Zac, leave! Get off him, you stupid twat! It's a fucking inspector!"

CHAPTER SIXTEEN

BITE FORCE

Bite force is the pressure of a creature's bite. For humans, it averages around 162 pounds per square inch, whereas for German Shepherds, it is approximately 238 ppsi. A crocodile has the most powerful bite, the highest recorded bite being 3700 ppsi, so my earlier statement about Blue's bite being like a crocodile's wasn't quite accurate only being 3,462 ppsi out.

Although it would be awesome to have a police crocodile, finding vans big enough for them would be a bit of an issue. So German Shepherds will have to suffice. Shouting a challenge of "Stand still or I'll send the croc!" appealed to my sometimes bizarre sense of humour.

Other breeds of dog have been tried, but GSDs are the best all-round dog for police work, and 238 pounds per square inch is more than enough.

Throughout his career, Zac took a bite out of many foes who were all warned and given the opportunity to cease their criminal activities or surrender. I believe everyone should be given a chance; however, if they chose to confront me or my co-workers with violence, we needed to respond appropriately.

To put 238 ppsi in perspective, one night I attended a garden centre due to a report of intruders on the premises. At the rear of the large building where I found it had been broken into, Zac immediately pulled me up a hill, indicating a line of scent. Reaching the top of the hill, he indicated a gate out onto the road, where I saw two colleagues. They said they hadn't seen anybody so my initial thought was that the villain or villains must have got out onto the road, evading capture.

However, Zac's nose began twitching in the direction of a tree and an adjacent bush, and with his ears pricked and hackles rising he was telling me that someone was nearby. I shouted for them to come out, and as no answer came, I released Zac from his lead. He dived under the tree and into the bush beyond, and soon enough dragged out a man by his arm, whom I arrested for burglary, handing him to my two colleagues at the gate.

After the incident, he had to be taken to hospital, where not only did they fix his wound with stitches but also X-rayed him, revealing a broken arm. Imagine what kind of destruction a police crocodile would have caused!

Another instance of a dog's bite power was a situation that involved another police dog.

Early one morning, when I was on the night shift, I was meant to meet my friend Andy from the Halifax division at Lindley Moor around 5:15 in the morning so our dogs could run around before we headed home. When I arrived a few minutes late, Andy was shouting and frantically looking for his four-legged companion; he had lost his dog, Sam, and despite searching for him, he was nowhere to be seen.

We set out to find him, scanning the area with our torches, and within a few minutes, we spotted him running along the quiet road that cut through the bottom of the moor. This road was mostly deserted, with only a handful of houses along its length. Coincidentally, one of those homes belonged to a high-ranking police superintendent who also served as the assistant divisional officer in Andy's division.

Having got hold of Sam and done our walk, Andy and his dog left Zac and me, seemingly without a care in the world, but the next evening Andy contacted me via radio, asking me to meet him on the moor. There, he informed me that after leaving me that morning, he had driven past the superintendent's house and had come upon a dead sheep with its throat ripped open. When I asked what he did with it, he answered – sheepishly – "Nothing. I drove around it and went home." He asked me not to tell anyone, so being a good friend, I kept it secret … well, for at least a few hours.

Years later, Andy and Sam were presented with a divisional officers award, with a local newspaper capturing the moment on camera. A lovely photo of Andy, Sam and the assistant divisional officer all pictured in the local rag.

I decided to have some fun with the snapshot, and drew a thought bubble coming from Sam that said: "I wonder if this guy knows it was me who killed the sheep outside his house?" After photocopying it, I posted it all around the dog training school and kennels. Plus, I might have also mailed out copies to every dog section office. Andy should have known better than to ask me not to tell anyone about this. I also wondered if the assistant divisional officer may have seen a copy.

CHAPTER SEVENTEEN

GROUP 2

In the late eighties and early nineties, all of the older, "Nowt here for me, kid" handlers had retired or moved on, making way for a new generation of fit and eager officers in the section.

There were ten of us in the Division, all highly dedicated to our jobs of assisting other police officers in their work to catch criminals. A few of them also took part in dog trials, never letting this get in the way of their primary duties. I was given the honour of tutoring some of these new handlers, and through those experiences, I made some lasting friendships.

Around this time our shift patterns changed to align with the rest of the division. I was assigned to work with group 2 in the Huddersfield Town Centre and outer sub-divisions. Working with the same people, each shift was much more beneficial for me as it enabled everyone to become familiar with my skills, as well as what they could expect from us both as a team. Working with Group 2 was the best years of my dog-handling career; I met some terrific colleagues and Zac and I became integral members of the team. There were some amazing characters in our group, and many of us are still connected either via social media or through reunions at local pubs.

The team was educated to know that if I was attending a scene, they should not enter a building or run around searching for themselves, creating additional odours. Lots of successful arrests were made, not only due to the part Zac and I played but also our collaboration as a unit. Additionally, Zac's presence also served them in more confrontational encounters.

The first time these colleagues saw Zac in a really violent situation was a man brandishing a large knife, threatening them. They could not get near him as he swiped the blade back and forth towards them, standing in front of a low wall and flower bed that blocked any attempt to approach from behind. When I arrived with Zac, he immediately displayed aggression towards the commotion, so I approached first, whipping out my truncheon and commanding the assailant to drop the knife. The adrenaline, noise and highly charged emotions created a really tense atmosphere, and as I got closer, the officers parted like the Red Sea, allowing me to go forward with Zac, giving him full rein to attack. The man shouted that he would kill the dog, to which, unsurprisingly, Zac took offence and he bit into him fiercely; I followed, aiming a strike towards his shoulder with my truncheon, which ended up connecting with his head, making him collapse and drop the knife.

The rest of the shift then piled onto us atop the flower bed until he stopped moving, was eventually arrested and handcuffed once Zac had released him.

Later, we were acknowledged for our efforts and rewarded with a commendation. This event was one of many that established Zac's credibility within the Division and reminded many of the officers of the value of a well-trained police dog.

I heard more than once from officers that they had given up using dogs to investigate various incidents because all they ever got was the "Nowt here for me, kid" handlers, some of whom wouldn't even get out of the van, preferring to deliver the message through an open window.

One of these sceptical cops was at the scene of a stolen vehicle crash, with the thief having cleared off. I attached Zac to the harness and cast him around the car to search for any scent. The trail was quickly picked up and we began to follow. Finding some stolen property from the car confirmed we were on the right track, which led us over main roads, through a wooded area, allotments, and a disused railway line until we emerged at the back of several houses. Zac began to take great interest in one particular residence, sniffing around the steps and door. Its occupant was a well-known teenage car thief and burglar so my colleague knocked on the door, and sure enough, there stood a sweat-drenched and unkempt teenage car thief who was arrested for motor vehicle theft. He soon confessed to the offence, and I had the pleasure of arresting him twice more within a month, both times for burglary.

Zac astounded the police officer with his ability to follow the scent for over a mile-and-a-half, straight to the home of the thief. Of all the successful tracks we had throughout his working life, this one was exceptional. His tracking skills were gaining recognition, not only with our own team but also at the dog training school.

The easiest track we ever followed was at the scene of a burglary on one of the more threatening estates in our division. I could have left Zac resting in the van as we began to follow a set of deep footprints in the newly fallen snow, which led to a nearby dwelling where we encountered a young man of, shall we say, limited intelligence.

He proclaimed his innocence, but not only were his wet shoes in the hallway, we also followed the same tracks into his backyard and found the stolen items inside a rabbit hutch, minus the rabbit itself.

Sergeant Nev nominated me for a further commendation for another violent event, a reported domestic dispute. A man, absent without leave from the army, had assaulted his wife and was now alone, barricaded in their home, threatening to blow it up by putting the gas on and starting a fire. He also stated that he had a gun and would shoot anybody who tried to enter. I witnessed him at an open upstairs window, screaming out while waving a knife and a flickering lighter.

A firearms team were summoned as more officers attended to cordon off the house, and I waited by the back of my van, ready to take Zac out if things escalated. Wow, did it escalate! Moments later, flames engulfed the bedroom. Don, the inspector on the scene, kicked in the side door, and I was first in with Zac.

Reaching the top of the stairs, the front bedroom was well

alight, with smoke already seeping onto the landing. I heard someone in the room on my left, and as I entered, he rushed towards me with a knife in each hand, at which Zac leapt forward, biting him before he could attack us. I aimed at his shoulder with my truncheon, but missed the target again. Nonetheless, it knocked him down instantly, and he dropped the knives as he fell.

The inspector and sergeant grabbed the suspect while I managed to get Zac to release him. During the melee, Zac bit the sergeant on the hand – oops, another copper bitten, although not seriously.

As if the situation wasn't serious enough, the house was quickly filling with smoke, despite somebody closing the bedroom door. We exited quickly, leaving the fire brigade to extinguish the fire. As I returned Zac to the van with a big hug, Inspector Don shook my hand and congratulated me on the successful outcome of a really dangerous incident. Thankfully, no firearms were found in the house.

Later, all involved received a Crown Court judge's commendation for entering a burning building to arrest an armed and unstable suspect. These kinds of incidents just further improved our section's reputation, with some of my fellow dog handlers also performing commendable work.

I continued to work with Zac, determined not to let our successes go to my head. We went out on many unsuccessful missions, but I knew that Zac was never wrong – if there was someone hiding in a building or woods, we'd find them. The confidence and bond between us grew considerably greater.

At least once a year, we had to attend a two-week refresher course. Having heard of Zac's tracking prowess the instructor, Scotty, was very interested in testing his abilities by setting up a challenging track for him.

I was given a scenario and area where a suspect was last seen. I buckled Zac into his harness, and he immediately picked up the scent. We continued along the back wall of a huge metal structure, covered with a canvas-like material.

About halfway down the path, Zac stopped as if he had lost the scent, but then he pointed his nose up at a large L-shaped rip in the canvas wall of the building. I trusted in his ability and climbed through the hole into the building with him, where the track continued until we reached a yard, carrying on until he found his prize at the end of the trail.

The track was roughly half a mile long and covered a combination of different surfaces: concrete, asphalt, gravel and grass. Scotty was coming up for retirement and had been working as a dog handler for over two decades. He said it was the best track he'd ever seen worked by a dog, high praise from such a renowned handler!

Our shift pattern dictated that we worked one week of night shift once every four weeks, with nights being our busiest times. On one particular nights week, Zac and I arrested ten wrongdoers for a range of offences, including burglary and car theft among others, and also found a large amount of stolen property.

I was directed to a burglary taking place in a less than salubrious area of the Division, along with the make and number of a car seen driving away from the scene. It was suspected that there were four occupants, including one notorious criminal who had absconded from prison some six months prior.

Nearing the scene, I noticed the car going in the opposite direction and radioed my fellow officers, simultaneously performing a screeching hand-brake turn to pursue the suspects!

I activated the entire display of blues and twos, which always triggered Zac into whining and howling as his adrenaline started pumping. The car came to a sudden halt near a golf club, and all four men jumped from it, scattering in different directions. I swiftly removed Zac and sprinted towards the only man I could still see.

Commands to stop went unheeded, so I released Zac to chase him. He set off with his usual air of confidence, across a car park and over a main road before catching up with him. He was ready to launch himself when the man turned quickly, swinging a baseball bat and hitting Zac squarely across his front legs and then across his head, causing him to drop to the floor, giving the villain time to disappear from view. By the time I caught up with Zac, he had picked himself up, appearing slightly dazed, and was looking around for the runner. We continued, turning into a narrow lane where the bastard was standing, breathless, brandishing the bat again, but before he could swing another blow, Zac lunged at him, biting his arm with his full 328 ppsi … plus a little extra. We struggled as I managed to wrestle the bat from him and, with help from two traffic officers, subdued him on the ground. When I released Zac, he kicked out, which prompted Zac to bite his leg, just for good measure! He was taken away while I returned to the abandoned car to continue the search.

I noticed Zac had a slight limp as we made our way back, yet he still appeared furious at being struck with the bat. The same anger was raging within me, too.

When I arrived back at the car, I liaised with a colleague who was searching it, and this is where good teamwork is paramount. He knew not to go searching by himself as he understood he could be spreading more scent, which could confuse the dog, so what happened next was also down to him as well as Zac.

We went into the golf club, where Zac was quickly hot on the scent across the course. We followed it across fairways, over a green, and at one point through a bunker, where it looked like the baddie had taken a tumble. We eventually reached the woods on the far side of the course, and on reaching the tree line, Zac gave me the indication I had seen many times, telling me someone was very near. He then told me in his own unique way, "I've got this, Dad, let me go," which of course I did. Oops, I forgot to give him the opportunity to come out first, which must have been the adrenaline still coursing around my body, causing a brain malfunction. After what could have been only a few seconds, there was a bloodcurdling scream as Zac had obviously found his quarry, duly handing out his own form of justice. Whilst escorting the imbecile back to my colleagues, he swore up and down he was blameless. He asked why he had been arrested, claiming all he was doing was taking a casual stroll through the woods! For a whole nanosecond I considered believing him but not raking the bunker was still a crime in my eyes, so that was enough evidence to arrest him. Once again, another dimwit requiring stitches and a tetanus injection.

The other two individuals who fled the scene were apprehended by colleagues. It was a brilliant outcome overall, with the criminal from HMP (who had struck Zac) sent back behind bars to face not only a fresh term of imprisonment but also the remainder of his old sentence.

For this incident, we were awarded West Yorkshire's Police Dog Handler of the Year and were shortlisted for National Police Dog Handler of the Year, which was ultimately awarded to a dog that had been stabbed in the line of duty, understandably deserving of the award, however, we were highly commended.

Despite being whacked with the bat, Zac soon shrugged off any pain and was fit for duty; I, on the other hand, needed a cuppa followed by a good lie down!

The following night, I was driving to another burglary where three men had been disturbed in the act. Two of them had run away, while the third sped off in a car. Luckily for us, a witness got the registration number, and as fate would have it, I spotted the vehicle heading in the opposite direction as I drove towards my destination. I got a feeling of déjà vu as I swiftly executed a U-turn and chased after it until it entered the grounds of a school near the woods where the previous night's incident had occurred.

The driver of the car hit the brakes, leapt out, and scurried off into the woods. I let Zac out of the van; no orders were necessary, and he was gone in an instant. The same scenario as the previous night followed, and a few seconds later there was a loud yell, then capture, and ultimately a visit to the A&E department for stitches.

As it happened, they would be receiving another customer very shortly …

I was asked to meet two officers on an industrial estate near the burglary, and on arrival, I was met by PCs Trevor and John. (The same John who refused to hold the lead when I was fighting with Blue many moons before.)

We formulated a plan to capture the two missing burglars by using their car as a Trojan horse. I got on the back seat with Zac, and, with Trevor driving, we drove into the area of the offence, hoping they would break cover. Well, it wasn't long before the two came out of hiding and started running up the road towards us. I was struggling to contain the excitement and was also trying not to piss myself laughing as they got closer.

I quickly checked to see if Trevor had forgotten to take his police cap off as the two seemed to realise it wasn't their mate and quickly jumped over a wall into a field. Zac was straight out, over the wall almost immediately, sending another to

A&E, at which his burgling mate stood up, hands in the air, obviously not wanting 'Zacking' – a wise move. A colleague informed me that Zac had become a topic of conversation among the A&E nurses on duty that week. I hoped they were sticking the tetanus injection slow and hard into the burglars' arse cheeks.

Another terrific job, so back to the nick in time for tea, cakes, plenty of pats on the back, and a frame of snooker with John; could life get any better? Of course it could, but not right at that very moment.

A few more successful jobs resulting in arrests made this the standout week in my 30-year career.

Due to the location of our outer sub-divisions, we were getting a number of villains travelling into our area from neighbouring forces.

One such incident was a report of burglars at one of our more remote villages near the border with Greater Manchester, which was unusual as it was a daytime burglary. When I arrived, I was told that one youth had been arrested, but there was another who had evaded capture by jumping in the river. I was searching the canal area near where he had last been seen, and it wasn't long before I saw the suspect on the canal tow path about 100 yards away from me. I released Zac after he decided to ignore my command to stop.

Usain Bolt could sprint a hundred yards in less than ten seconds, yet Zac could make the same distance in around half that time. Before long, he was nearly upon the lad, who stopped, seemingly unsure whether to dive into the canal or not.

Whatever he was thinking, it was too late, and Zac arrested him swiftly. I noticed he was dressed in a school uniform that was absolutely soaked. It transpired that he and his friend had skipped school and come across the Pennines on the bus to burgle some houses. Both of them were only 16 years old.

Both kids' parents had to drive from Manchester to collect them. The mother of the lad whom Zac apprehended was not pleased; in fact, she was fuming. She grabbed the bag filled with her son's property, and while exiting the station, she pulled out his belt and began thrashing him with it, using some foul expletives as she did so. None of us witnessed that of course (okay, we did), but we can only imagine how embarrassed he was: getting piss wet through by jumping in the river, bitten by a police dog, and then thrashed by his mum using his own belt.

Maybe staying at school for double maths would have been a better option.

Another burglar, from Barnsley, must have wished that he had stayed in his hometown, too. He had targeted a local club in a quiet hamlet of the Division, and on my arrival, I was told that the intruder had left the premises, having attacked the slot machine, stealing the cash as well as the cigarette machine.

Just over the river from the club was a church and graveyard. I called out for anyone to come out of hiding, but got no reply. Zac seemed particularly alert, leading me to believe that perhaps someone was hiding nearby. Sure enough, shortly thereafter, Zac leapt over the wall of the cemetery and was soon pulling Burgling Barnsley Bill from behind a gravestone.

Another perp who should have given himself up, stayed home in Barnsley, or better yet, stopped burgling. He was arrested and handed over to other officers at the scene while I continued the search.

Zac indicated something, sniffing over a wall towards the riverbank. He jumped up with his front feet on top of the wall, pointing his nose towards a plastic bag dangling on the branch of a tree overhanging the river bank. Although we could have got over the wall, it was too steep and precarious down to the river.

My friend, Daring Derek, was at the scene and came to see if he could reach and retrieve the bag. He scaled the wall, perilously holding onto a tree as he reached out to get the bag, and as he took hold of it, he called out that the bag was full of pound coins. As he attempted to remove it from the tree limb, the bag split open, and all we could hear was a rapid plink, plink, and more plinks as around £250 worth of shiny golden coins tumbled down into the River Holme. We stared at each other in disbelief before bursting into laughter at our mishap. There's a good chance that those coins are still there, waiting to be retrieved by a trout tickler. The cigarette machine and its carcinogenic contents were found just over the wall, near to where Derek had launched the coins into the water.

We were once sent to an interesting yet amusing incident: persons breaking into the pavilion in a place close to my and many Huddersfield officers' hearts: the Police Sports Ground, Woodfield Park, a spectacular area boasting a football pitch, cricket field, tennis courts and a bowling green, approximately two miles from the divisional HQ. The land had been gifted to Huddersfield Borough Police years ago, and as a way of honouring that commitment, there was an annual football match played between CID and Road Traffic Officers. I took part in that competitive contest many times, playing for the Road Traffic team.

I cherish the many memories of playing football and cricket for the divisional teams there. We would also take our dogs to get some exercise and sometimes do training sessions. Additionally, I spent lots of quality time with my family, attending numerous events hosted by the sports and social club, such as bonfires and other social get-togethers.

The police station also had a bar run by the sports and social club, complete with a snooker table. I played snooker for the Division in a local league for decades. Years later, however, the police hierarchy sold Woodfield Park and shut down all police station bars, huge mistakes in my opinion. Not only did they offer a refuge from the pressures of policing, but also bred team-building and provided an avenue for solving crimes through information exchange. Woodfield Park is now derelict and overgrown, breaking my heart every time I drive by, as I remember all the hours spent playing sports, time spent with family, and socialising.

Anyway, I digress, so I'll stop dreaming of the halcyon days and get back to the incident.

When I arrived, there was a traffic car blocking the driveway, so I had to leave the van on the main road. As I sprinted closer, a voice bellowed, "Freeze, or I'll send the dog!" followed by an intense bout of deep-throated barking.

This confused me as I thought I was the only dog handler working that night. As I approached the back of the pavilion, I saw a traffic man, Dave, shining his torch on three youths, spread-eagled, face down, on the bowling green. He was doing a brilliant impression of a frenzied police dog barking at them. I arrived, allowing Dave and his throat a break as Zac took over the barking.

More officers joined us, and Police Dog Dave arrested the three suspects who were completely oblivious to what had caused their capture.

Dave later received some recognition for this job: a bollocking from a senior officer for going on his own and not waiting for backup. In my opinion, he should have received some formal award for good police work, using his initiative, or at least been nominated for "The Police Dog of the Year Award." Had he not taken the action he did, three burglars would have had the chance to escape, one of them a prolific burglar and thief whom I had the pleasure of arresting on more than one occasion.

Throughout the years working with Group 2, we made lots of arrests and assisted with many more, providing support for the shift during lots of varied, sometimes amusing incidents, as well as violent events.

Zac had already taken a bite out of two officers, a sergeant and Inspector Mick, and then along came the third – a detective. My assignment was to search a wooded area near the town centre for a daytime burglar who had been spotted entering the wood with a stolen television. Before I released Zac, I radioed the other officers to get out of the woods. All of them responded that they'd heard me and understood. Clearly, the detective outside of our group either didn't understand, didn't listen, or just assumed that Zac would recognise him because of his traditional detective attire or superior aura.

I let Zac go, sprinting off in his usual energetic way. He ran towards a high wall near a building surrounded by trees where I noticed another detective, Alan, at the top of the wall. When I asked him if he had seen anyone, he just shook his head with a resounding "No". Suddenly, Zac stopped, turned left out of view, and started barking loudly before a male voice shouted out "Get him off!" When I got to the end of the wall, I saw that he was attacking a detective. It was odd that he wasn't just pulling or holding on to him as would be his usual modus operandi; instead, he kept letting go and then trying to bite again as the innocent detective tried to waft him away with flailing arms. Alan had now arrived and was absolutely cracking up at the sight of his CID colleague being mauled. We never caught the perpetrator, but we did recover the TV.

This incident was the main topic of conversation the following evening at the annual CID versus Road Traffic football match, during which I made sure I was in a different area of the pitch from the aggrieved, well-bruised detective.

Zac was trained regularly, fine-tuning his skills and working diligently until in his tenth year when his age began to catch up with him.

His responses to commands were slower, and he became less agile, which were reasons for my decision to retire him.

Planning to fill the void after Zac was to retire, I adopted a six-month-old German Shepherd. He was solid black with no markings whatsoever, except for his massive tongue and his pink lipstick, which only made an appearance when he was excited. His pedigree certificate had another fucking stupid name that didn't suit him at all, so I gave him the more fitting handle of Jet. I'm pretty sure Baron Von Shithousen wasn't included on that certificate anyway, which means he wasn't related to Zac. Big Bob and Vinny would surely have known, but they had both retired by then, and, if I'm honest, I didn't care.

I was grateful to Sergeant Nev for helping me plan Jet's education. Although I devoted much of my time to this programme, I kept working with Zac, who, despite his age-related physical decline, still had an enthusiasm for the job. I did, however, stop all training for him so he could conserve his energy for the important tasks.

Before he went into his well-deserved retirement, Zac had one last hurrah. I was called to help Road Traffic, who had pulled over a vehicle with possible cloned licence plates.

There were three suspects, and one of them I recognised. He was one of the first arrests Zac had made years before, someone he'd found hiding by a canal after having committed an assault. Coincidentally he was also the first individual whom Zac had had the pleasure of biting after the man reacted irately when more cops turned up, although to be fair it was more of a nip.

I warned the traffic officers that the suspect would either fight or run, so I went to get Zac out of the van in preparation for either outcome. As soon as I opened the door of the van, the man shot off, hopping over a wall into a large expanse of woodland. I followed with Zac, and as we jumped over the wall, I yelled at the offender to stop, to encourage my canine companion, but I didn't need to; Zac knew exactly what he had to do, even though he couldn't see his quarry at this point.

I watched as he detected something and veered off quickly to the right. Struggling to keep up, I entered a clearing and spotted Zac not far behind him. The baddie attempted to climb a tree but was too slow; Zac lunged towards him, grabbing his leg and yanking him down. As soon as he landed on the ground, Zac released his leg and took hold of his left arm.

It seemed a rush of energy had surged through the man's body as he began to spin around, Zac still hanging from his arm like a rag doll. His right fist crashed into Zac's head a number of times, but no matter how hard he thrashed and punched, he couldn't free himself from the grip.

However, he was showing a lot of strength and wouldn't go down, so I drew my truncheon and aimed a blow at his shoulder but as you already know, my aim has never been great. I caught him with a whack across his head, which dropped him like the proverbial sack of shit, and I then got on top, kneeling on him with Zac still holding his left arm.

As his adrenaline slowly faded, he began to yell, demanding that I remove the dog from his vice-like grip. My response was a defiant "No chance," or maybe some other expletives were used until my fellow Group 2 officers could get there to handcuff him and take him into custody. Another successful job. The other two occupants of the car were arrested after three ski masks and baseball bats were found in the car, clearly to be used for something more serious than playing a game of rounders in the snow! No doubt that a plan to commit a serious offence had been prevented by all the officers concerned, another example of great teamwork.

The man was later taken to hospital for treatment of bites to his leg and arm ... and a wound to an area somewhere near his shoulder.

CHAPTER EIGHTEEN

X-RAY 99

Sometime around 1989 or 1990, our force acquired a helicopter, call sign X-ray 99. It was the pride and joy of the force hierarchy and was based on the field outside the dog training school. I remember hoping that they had moved the shit buckets. I mean, can you imagine the carnage if the downdraught from the rotors sent them flying? It was housed in a large marquee used as a temporary hangar, and I was assigned, for one whole boring night, the tedious job of protecting it from any potential terrorists. Fortunately, Derek, who had recently been promoted to the rank of sergeant in a division near the training school, stopped by for an hour or so. We kept each other company with our usual wit and repartee, coffee and sandwiches, which made the night a lot more bearable. Sitting by the impressive chopper for most of the night, I fantasised about what scenarios it might be used for: would I see it in action, would I get a flight in it, or would it be a completely expensive white elephant? To answer the first two questions: "Yes" to both.

The first time I encountered the chopper in action was when I responded to a reported burglary in a remote village on the outskirts of the Division. On one of the recently constructed and smaller housing estates, there had been a break-in. When I arrived, it was around two o'clock in the morning, but the entire neighbourhood had already gathered outside, staring up towards the sky, wearing a whole range of nightwear: it was like an advert for Marks & Spencer. The loud whirring sound of the rotors was unmistakable, but the chopper also shone the brightest light ever into the woodland next to the estate. There was an infrared thermal camera mounted on it to detect body heat, but after a while, we heard over the radio that X-ray 99 couldn't locate anything and needed to refuel.

I decided I'd go ahead and send in my own heat seeker: Zac. He was on the lead as we entered the woods where he soon indicated, in his usual excitable way, that someone was skulking in the bushes nearby. I shone my not-so-bright torchlight into the darkness and saw Zac was barking fiercely at a youth desperately trying to hide in the foliage. Fortunately, there was no need for a 'Zacking' or a badly aimed truncheon strike on my part as the youth emerged from the shrubbery at my command.

I arrested him, securing the cuffs around his wrists, and with Zac prancing to my left side, I walked out of the woods, gripping him on my right. The crowd, still in their M&S night attire, clapped and cheered as we passed, causing me to take a bow. I drove away with a massive grin, feeling triumphant, thinking to myself that in spite of the millions spent on a police helicopter fitted with cutting-edge technology, it was a £30 police dog that had caught the thief in mere minutes, using its nose. You can decide which was better value for money.

I was invited to take a spin in the helicopter with Zac, for training purposes, in case we were ever needed in an emergency situation.

That seemed very unlikely, though; it felt like more of an excuse to have some fun. While a lot of the dogs shied away from the flight, Zac welcomed the chance to be up in the air, admiring the view below. The dog training school appeared so different from above; I spotted the shit buckets and wondered if they could be seen at night through the infrared heat-detecting camera.

As an instructor, I set up lots of different scenarios for dog teams to deal with. As part of one training exercise, the team would take a short flight and then jump out after landing, releasing their dog to chase down a fleeing man.

A health and safety risk assessment wouldn't allow them to jump out with a parachute or even abseil out, which would have been far more spectacular. However, it was still a blast for the dog, handler and pilot alike, although it probably wouldn't happen in 'real life'.

CHAPTER NINETEEN

RETIREMENT

After working diligently for around nine years, Zac was ready for retirement. We had collared over 250 criminals, recovered countless stolen items worth thousands of pounds, and received five commendations for courageous and exemplary police work. He consistently encountered the most threatening perpetrators, armed with bats, blades, and once even a broken bottle, never hesitating to put my well-being and that of my colleagues ahead of his own.

We had the honour of being named the West Yorkshire Police Dog and Handler Team of the Year for 1990. We had given and attended numerous public talks and displays, which made me so proud of what we'd achieved in terms of community relations. I was also proud to have contributed to improving the reputation of the police dog section by joining a team that worked to find criminals and keep both the public and police officers safe, and never once did I say, "Nowt here for me, kid."

I was proud of my time working with Group 2 as we had a great dynamic, and everyone adored Zac. To show their thanks for his years of service, they threw him a retirement party at a nearby pub.

Despite Zac's non-attendance, it was a retirement party full of laughs and reminiscences, and a joint celebration that included two members of the group who had recently got engaged.

I was determined to give Zac a comfortable retirement, even though the force policy remained unchanged. I applied for him to be retired as a pet, but I had to jump through more hoops than a display team obstacle course.

The powers that be were concerned that he might attack somebody and that the force might be dragged into a civil court dispute. I was advised by a number of people not to keep him, as he may be a liability and this could also affect Jet's training.

I was determined to keep my beloved Zac, despite any warnings against it, and I was prepared to take responsibility for the consequences of this decision. My family was attached to him, too; my son especially loved spending time with him, sitting in Zac's kennel, feeling comforted as he confided his stresses to his four-legged pal.

I wasn't concerned that he would become a dangerous animal, attempting to bite anyone in his path. Being trained to attack didn't automatically mean he would do so. His temperament was always good-natured and amicable, until he had to work.

After promising to take care of him, provide him with food, and take responsibility for any vet fees or incidents that happened thereafter, I signed a disclaimer and adopted Zac as my own.

We kept him as our pet and it was clear that he had earned the right to a dignified retirement. If he could, he would have been contentedly rocking on a chair with a pipe in his mouth and fluffy slippers on his feet. It was an honour to be able to take care of him during the remainder of his life; after all, he had taken such good care of me throughout the years, so I was eager to return the favour.

CHAPTER TWENTY

LIFE AFTER ZAXON

I spent over three years working with Jet, and although I had a great bond with him, it never compared to my time with Zac. His tracking ability was almost as good, and he received a commendation from a Crown Court judge for tracking from the scene of a grievous bodily harm case, where part of a man's ear had been bitten off. The track went for half a mile until it led to the door of the perpetrator, who was subsequently apprehended.

During my tenure with Jet, I received extensive training as a Police Advanced Pursuit Driver. This gruelling four-week course pushed me to the limit and challenged everything I thought I knew about driving. Driving at incredibly high speeds while still maintaining safety standards was a discipline in itself.

My newfound skills set allowed me to operate a specialised vehicle, a Volvo T5 car with custom dog cages, designed for pursuing car thieves, burglars, and other criminals who were rampant at the time. Fondly referred to as "the hotdog car," it was an absolute joy to drive.

One of my more macho friends kept telling me that he

had driven the hot-dog car at 150mph. I won't say who it was, but his dog had an appetite for mutton. I couldn't help but take him up on his inferred challenge and see what it felt like to drive at such speed. So, on one quiet night shift, I got onto the straightest part of an unusually empty M62 motorway and hit the pedal until I reached 150mph. Fucking hell, it was so fast! As soon as I hit that speed, I took my foot off the gas and promised myself never to do something so foolish again. So far, I've kept that promise; well, as regards driving, anyway.

We had a few successes in the hotdog car. On one sprint down Manchester Road, Huddersfield, while pursuing a stolen vehicle we tripped every single speed camera we passed; no way to tell how many there were, but I'd say at least ten. Even so, I never got points on my licence nor did I have to attend a speed awareness course. The driver was arrested after crashing the car, and, as he didn't want to get out, we removed him from the vehicle by forcing the door and letting Jet's teeth do the rest.

A few years later, I transferred my trusty police dog Jet to my sergeant at the time, Adrian. By that point, I was an instructor at the same training school I had started at two decades before and no longer needed a general-purpose dog. Though it was emotional parting with him, I knew Adrian would take good care of him. Jet quickly became accustomed to being fed by his new dad; this was proven when I acted as the criminal during a training session with Adrian. I appeared from hiding, waving a stick about and acting threateningly towards him. Jet didn't pause for even a moment, biting me with full force.

As part of my new role, I was responsible for training and working with Beth, a border collie who had an incredibly natural sense of smell, ideal for sniffing out explosives. She was also extremely controllable, which is essential for a bomb-detection dog. Fortunately, she never found any real bombs; it's probably the only job in the police service where you hope to have zero success.

The year 2003 marked the end of my 30 years of service as a policeman, 25 as a dog handler. My partner, Beth, retired with me and was part of our family for the rest of her life.

I can proudly say that I accomplished much during my time in the force, but nothing could compare to working with Zac, the most perfect partner anyone could have asked for.

I also think I proved Inspector "you're wasting your career" wrong, and I rammed the smarmy fucking training sergeant's words down his fucking smarmy throat.

I could have stayed in the force for six more years, but I felt like it was time to go. Police politics had become oppressive, with many higher-ranking supervisors becoming too politically correct for the job to be totally effective. It was apparent that they were making cutbacks as well; when I retired, the dog section had 56 handlers, and now it only has around half that. It's sad that such a valuable resource has been diminished.

Perhaps there aren't enough highly approachable police

officers who can empathise with the public, like Inspector Micks or Sergeant Nevs. Nonetheless, I feel a sense of pride in having worked as a policeman for 33 years, including my cadet service, contributing to the removal of some of the most abhorrent individuals from society, even if only for a brief time.

I would like to express my gratitude to all the people who have impacted both my life and time in the police service, be it in a positive or negative way. Special mentions go to Storm and Zeus, who taught me about the dogs that are fit for companionship but not for police work, and Blue, Jet and Beth for their services as well as their friendship.

Many thanks to Group 2 for accepting me into their fantastic gang, both professionally and socially, with plenty of good-natured, unadulterated humour.

My career provided countless thrilling yet dangerous and tragic experiences that tested my emotional boundaries; however, the joyous moments far outweighed the more stressful ones.

I've met people from all walks of life, some making lasting impressions, and others who … I'm sorry, I've forgotten them. I have made some friends whom I love and hold in high regard, being part of a close-knit police family.

THE FINAL CHAPTER

Zac was thirteen plus when he could no longer move freely. His back legs were struggling to operate, and he began to frequently fall down. One morning, I went to his kennel, and he remained lying down despite my encouragement. He looked straight into my eyes and it appeared he was telling me that it was time for the end. We had all been expecting it, but it was still difficult to make the call. We discussed it as a family and eventually decided to have him put to sleep.

I scheduled an appointment with the vet and drove him there later that day. There were no blue lights or sirens this time, just a short tranquil journey.

I spoke to him gently while he was being prepared, holding back my emotions. After the needle was inserted, the vet granted me a final gesture of affection: to push the syringe down and send him on his final journey. Zac looked up at me one last time before drifting off to his final sleep. My loyal police dog and best four-legged friend passed away peacefully and dignified. I had a couple of minutes alone with him before leaving for my car, where my emotions exploded.

A few weeks after his passing, we received his ashes and decided that Lindley Moor was the best place to scatter them. We waited for a day with lots of wind so the ashes would spread out as far as possible. All four of us went out onto the moor, and as I muttered something incomprehensible, I set Zac free, letting the strong gusts carry him fast and far away across the moor, something he had done many times before.

Once we returned home, I went into the garden, opened a beer and lit a cigar, reflecting on our time together. One of the kids came out, I can't remember which one, and said, "Mum wants you to come in." I downed the beer, extinguished my cheroot, and went in. I planned to go back out and repeat. When I went in, I was given a gift: a painted portrait of my beautiful Zac, which induced more tears. The picture still proudly adorns the wall in our living room. An emotional but wonderful day for us all.

Shortly after I had Zac put to sleep, I received a letter from Sergeant Nev. He praised my work alongside Zac, adding that not only had I fulfilled my obligation as a dog handler to Zac, but Zac had definitely fulfilled his obligation as a police dog, not only to me but also to the public of West Yorkshire.

    Wow! What more can I say? Nothing!

Printed in Great Britain
by Amazon